"Kim Adelman has not only taught me the nuts and bolts of short film-making, more importantly she gave me a strong sense of empowerment. Her words 'You are the studio' kept ringing in my ear while I was in the middle of shooting the short that set off my career."

> — Lexi Alexander, filmmaker, *Johnny Flynton* (2002 Academy Award nominee live action short)

"Kim Adelman has a breadth of knowledge that is unmatched in short film production. Her experience navigating international film festivals is invaluable to filmmakers."

> — Megan O'Neill, Director of Acquisitions, AtomShockwave

"This killer book is a must-read for any filmmaker currently working or looking to launch a career with shorts. Solid, important, and easy-to-digest instruction clearly explains what it takes to make a successful short film, find an audience, and profit from the experience."

> — Mark Steven Bosko, Author, *The Complete Independent Movie Marketing Handbook*

"*The Ultimate Filmmaker's Guide to Short Films* is required reading for all aspiring filmmakers, whether making their first short or their fiftieth. Written in a breezy, conversational style, the book is jam-packed with invaluable information and insider tips."

> — Shane Smith, Director, Canadian Film Centre's Worldwide Short Film Festival in Toronto

"There's a real need for a short film book, and Kim Adelman is the perfect person to write it."

> — Susan O'Leary, Director of Fox Searchlab

"The definitive guide to everything any short filmmaker needs to know. If this book had been around when I made my film, I would have done a lot better."

> — Noah Edelson, filmmaker, *"78"* (1997 S   Festival)

"Every year Kim Adelman shares her extensive knowledge of making and marketing the short film with UCLA Extension students. Now that knowledge can reach even more aspiring filmmakers via her book, *The Ultimate Filmmaker's Guide to Short Films: Making It Big in Shorts.*"

> — Jane Kagon, Director, Entertainment Studies Department, UCLA Extension

From concept to budgets, from legal rights to getting the most out of the festival circuit, Kim Adelman covers absolutely everything you will need to know when it comes to making a "short," and she does it in such an entertaining and insightful way. But the best-kept secret about *The Ultimate Filmmaker's Guide to Short Films* is that so much of what she covers can be applied to making it in television, cable, and theatrical features as well!

> — Kathie Fong Yoneda, Paramount Pictures story analyst/development specialist & author of *The Script-Selling Game*

"Kim Adelman's expertise flows through the pages of this must-have short film guide. This short film bible is sure to propel short filmmakers along to make better films, and movies that will have the ABCs in place for commercial success."

> — Douglas Williams, Creative Director, Short Shorts Film Festival

"Kim Adelman knows her stuff. A much needed guide to the underground world of short films."

> — David Birdsell, filmmaker, *Bad Animals* (2001 International Critics Week, Cannes)

"Who knew there was so much to say about shorts?! Kim Adelman's new *The Ultimate Filmmaker's Guide to Short Films* is just that — a virtual encyclopedia on the subject, chock full of practical real-world advice that will appeal to filmmakers of all types and all genres. This mini-course in every aspect of the topic is sure to make filmmakers devoted to shorts stand tall for years to come."

> — Morrie Warshawski, Author, *Shaking the Money Tree: How to Get Grants and Donations for Film and Television*

MICHAEL WIESE PRODUCTIONS
www.mwp.com

We are delighted that you have found and are enjoying our books.

Since 1981 we've been all about providing filmmakers with the very best information on the craft of filmmaking: from screenwriting to funding, from directing to camera, acting, editing, distribution and new media.

It's our goal to inspire and empower a generation (or two) of film and videomakers like yourself. But we want to go beyond providing you just with the basics. We want to shake you, and inspire you, to reach for your dreams and go beyond what's been done before. Most films that come out each year waste our time and enslave our imagination. We want to give you the confidence to create from your authentic center, to bring something from your own experience which will truly inspire others and bring humanity to its full potential — avoiding those urges to manufacture derivative work in order to be accepted.

Movies, television, the Internet, and new media all have incredible power to transform. As you prepare your next project, know that it is in your hands to choose to create something magnificent and enduring for generations to come.

This is not an impossible goal because you've got a little help. Our authors are some of the most creative mentors in the business, willing to share their hard-earned insights with you. Their books will point you in the right direction but ultimately it's up to you to seek that authentic something on which to spend your precious time.

We applaud your efforts and are here to support you. Let us hear from you.

Sincerely,

Michael Wiese
Filmmaker, Publisher

THE ULTIMATE FILMMAKER'S GUIDE TO SHORT FILMS

MAKING IT BIG IN SHORTS

KIM ADELMAN

Published by Michael Wiese Productions
11288 Ventura Blvd., Suite 621
Studio City, CA 91604
tel. (818) 379-8799
fax (818) 986-3408
mw@mwp.com
www.mwp.com

Cover design: Barry Grimes
Book layout: William Morosi
Editor: Paul Norlen
Index: Bruce Tracy, Ph.D

Printed by McNaughton & Gunn, Inc., Saline, Michigan
Manufactured in the United States of America

Library of Congress Cataloging-in-Publication Data

Adelman, Kim
  The ultimate filmmaker's guide to short films : making it big in
shorts / by Kim Adelman.
      p. cm.
Includes index.
  ISBN 0-941188-89-2
  1. Motion pictures--Production and direction. 2. Short films. I.
Title.
PN1995.9.P7 A35 2004
791.4302'3--dc22

CONTENTS

PART III: MARKETING YOUR FILM

FOREWORD

BY

MARK BORCHARDT

When I was growing up, I'd say to people, "Hey, man, I want to make a film about this dude delivering newspapers." And they'd laugh and say, "You're not making a movie, you're making something about yourself." Their idea of a movie was drug lords with machine guns and dark sunglasses. That's what qualifies as subject matter for films. Which is bull. Obviously.

Think for yourself. Give your own ideas birth. Time goes by so quickly that you really need to stop and think clearly about what you're doing. Don't let other people and situations dissuade you from your goals.

Listen, man, I was living in my parents' basement, drinking vodka or Pabst every day. At the age of twenty-seven, I said, "My God, this has to change. It has to change." And I spent three years making *Coven*.

I specifically made *Coven* as a short film because of financial restrictions and because I had no more story to tell. I didn't set out to make a short — I would have loved to make a feature. Finances and a very compact story informed the length.

But when you make a short film, the world is yours. Any idea goes. You're not regimented to any structure. When you make a feature film, you lose a certain amount of freedom. A feature has a sense of pace you must — you must! —adhere to, and that can get sticky and complicated in the crafting of the story. Whereas a short, man, a short can ride on a singular idea without the fabric of multiple plot twists, subplots, and secondary characters. It can be a single, flaming, meteoric idea.

That's a short film, man. A meteor going through the sky.

■ ■ ■

In 1980, fourteen-year-old Mark Borchardt paid forty dollars for his first movie camera, a Super-8. Borchardt's thirty-seven minute 16mm short, Coven, *has sold over 5,000 copies worldwide.* Coven *is available personally autographed on videotape at www.northwestproductions.com or as a bonus feature on the DVD version of the acclaimed documentary,* American Movie.

INTRODUCTION

"Call Kim," my friends and acquaintances eagerly counsel filmmakers who are about to make their first short. "Kim will tell you everything you need to know."

Thanks to increasingly accessible and affordable filmmaking tools, more and more aspiring auteurs are working outside the structured environment of film school and don't know whom to turn to for practical advice. "Call Kim" seems to be the answer. Why me? Because for four years I ran the short film program for the Fox Movie Channel. During the course of producing nineteen short films that played over one hundred and fifty film festivals worldwide and won thirty-plus awards, I learned a lot about the short film world. After the Fox program closed down, I joined a company that produced a series of acclaimed short film collections issued on DVD by Warner Home Video. Recording hours of director commentaries for the *Short* and *International Release* DVDs exposed me to even more insider information on the short filmmaking process. Meanwhile, the phone calls from knowledge-hungry aspiring filmmakers kept coming, so I created a course for UCLA Extension's Department of Entertainment Studies and Performing Arts entitled "Making and Marketing the Short Film." I also continued to appear on panels at film festivals to download everything I knew to directors desperately trying to figure out what to do with their short once it finished the festival circuit. One year when I was moderating a panel at the Palm Springs International Festival of Short Films, a frustrated audience member yelled out, "Why isn't any of this information written down anywhere?"

As you have probably discovered, there are many books written about the various aspects of movie making, but they're geared toward feature-length work. Although the basics of filmmaking are the same, there is a world of difference between making and marketing a ten-minute long piece versus a two-hour opus. The few books that do focus on shorts often don't address the primary concern of directors who have invested time, money, and dreams into their project: what to do after the short is done. Do you need to strike a print to play the festivals? Should you put your film on the Internet? And how do you parlay your short film into a well-paid career?

In reality, the truly helpful information is passed on from filmmaker to filmmaker in the form of insider tips from veterans to newcomers. I learned how to make successful shorts from two directors who had great success with their films. I shared my knowledge with the directors who worked with me in the Fox Movie Channel program. These Fox directors are now shooting commercials in the U.S. and in Europe, writing indie and Hollywood movies, manning second unit on big budget blockbusters, helming feature-length documentaries, writing and directing episodic television, and most impressively making more short films (one of which was nominated for an Oscar).

"Why isn't any of this information written down anywhere?" asked the frustrated filmmaker. Now it is. In putting together this book, I asked a host of experienced directors and industry experts to share their hard-won wisdom. Everything we know about the artistic and business sides of short form filmmaking is in this book. We'll tell you the unvarnished truth (including when to lie). After powering through *The Ultimate Filmmaker's Guide to Short Films: Making It Big in Shorts*, you, too, will know how to successfully make, exhibit, and sell a film of limited length in today's marketplace.

The Ultimate Filmmaker's Guide to Short Films is divided into three parts. The first section, Welcome to the Short Film World, will help you make an educated decision about what kind of film you should make. In these first six chapters, we'll cover what defines a short film, what defines a *good*

short film, whether you should consider going to film school, how to raise production money, and why you should or shouldn't join the digital video revolution. Each chapter ends with a recap of five important points to keep in mind as you embark on your filmmaking adventure.

The next section, Making Your Film, is a hands-on, step-by-step guide from story development through postproduction, with extensive advice from the trenches. You'll learn how to avoid the two things that ruin most shorts (bad acting and bad sound) and the two things that can cripple your film when you're ready to market it (SAG agreements and festival-only music licenses).

The final section, Marketing Your Film, focuses on what to do with your finished film, with inside information about how to get into the best festivals, how to get a distributor, how to make money off your film in the domestic and international marketplace, and how to parlay your short into a career. As you'll discover, there are a lot of essential "how-tos" in this guide!

"Kim not only taught me the nuts and bolts of short filmmaking, more importantly she gave me a strong sense of empowerment," proclaims Lexi Alexander, a student who took my short film class in 2002 and then went on to direct the Oscar-nominated live action short, *Johnny Flynton*. "Her words 'You are the studio' kept ringing in my ear while I was in the middle of shooting the short that set off my career."

The goal of *The Ultimate Filmmaker's Guide to Short Films* is to empower each and every one of you to go out and make an amazing film that will set off your career. Are you ready? Let's get started!

PART I:

WELCOME TO THE SHORT FILM WORLD

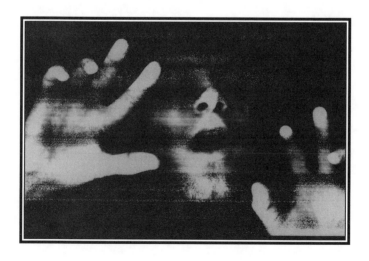

CHAPTER 1

SO YOU WANT TO MAKE A SHORT

All you need is motivation and money.

Celebrating his twelfth Academy Award nomination (for his performance in *About Schmidt*), Jack Nicholson confessed a shocking secret desire. Jack Nicholson — of *Easy Rider, One Flew Over the Cuckoo's Nest,* and *The Shining* fame — wished he could come up with an idea for a great short film. Even Jack Nicholson is not immune to the lure of short filmmaking! Of course, in Nicholson's case, it isn't surprising. Sure, he's a big old movie star. But he's also a graduate of the Roger Corman school of filmmaking, a longtime reader of O. Henry stories, and a fan of the student films that play on the Independent Film Channel.

What's stopping Mr. Nicholson from making a short? Certainly it isn't money. Although that's the major stumbling block for most wannabes, all Jack would have to do is put his courtside Lakers seats on eBay and he'd have instant funding for a pretty swanky little film. And it isn't because he doesn't have any ideas. Jack's been around long enough to know that ideas come to you all the time. No, Nicholson won't be making a short any time soon because he has too much respect for the format. Acknowledging that making a good short is something to be proud of, Jack is going to stay out of the pool rather than recklessly jumping in feet first to see what kind of splash he might make.

COME ON, IT'S EASY

In this new digital era, making a short is absurdly easy. First, you need to come up with an idea. Easy. Next, you have to round up the necessary people, places, and things to turn your idea into a reality. Also easy. Then, instead of having to pull strings to borrow a film camera, beg for free film stock, plead for discounted processing, and pray for gratis telecine like they used to do in the old days, all you have to do is get your hands on a digital video camera and some tape. With the proliferation of desktop editing systems, postproduction is also a breeze.

The most crucial ingredient is this: a burning passion to make a film. "One of the most common excuses for not making a short is claiming you don't have the right toys," suggests filmmaker Robbie Consing. "I always thought I can't do this unless I buy a Canon XL1, unless I have an iMac. Well, I bought those things, and I haven't done a short since!"

Luckily, you're not like Robbie. You're motivated. You're going to make a film. Now here's the bad news: It's so easy to make a short film in this new era that everyone's doing it. In 2003, the Sundance Film Festival programmers were amazed to discover that the number of short films submitted to the festival increased over forty percent from the previous year.

As those thousands of Sundance hopefuls discovered, the hard part is not getting an idea, assembling the toys, or getting passionately motivated. The hard part, as Jack Nicholson wisely pointed out, is making a short you can be proud of. Almost every filmmaker adds an apologetic commentary when showing their work: "The sound isn't quite right here," or "I wish I had moved the camera more in this sequence," or "I know she's no Meryl Streep, but my sister isn't half bad in this scene, don't you think?"

Forget about minor disappointments. Think big picture. Just making a short is a big accomplishment. You've crossed the treacherous bridge that many never traverse: On one side are those who want to be filmmakers but haven't yet made anything, on the other side are those who have made a short and therefore are filmmakers.

What's amazing is there is no one to stop you from crossing that bridge. You don't need an official piece of paper such as a license or a diploma. You don't need a "greenlight" from the head of a major motion picture studio. You don't even need to be related to Francis Ford Coppola (although that never hurts). You just need to get hold of a camera, run some film (or video) through it, give your piece a title, and you've done it. In fact, the very first motion picture by the Lumière Brothers in 1895 was essentially that. To mark the centennial anniversary of that achievement, forty acclaimed feature filmmakers such as Wim Wenders, David Lynch, Spike Lee, and Peter Greenaway took a turn at running fifty-two seconds of film through the original hand-cranked Lumière camera. You can check out the results on the DVD *Lumière & Company* (Fox Lorber Home Video, 1997). Truth be told, most of the pieces made by these modern masters aren't ground-shakingly amazing — once again proving that making a good short is a lot harder than you'd think!

EVERYONE IS WELCOME TO GIVE IT A TRY

Are you very old? Very young? Female? Asian? Disabled? Gay? Great! While Hollywood may practice ageism, sexism, or racism when it comes to hiring filmmakers to helm studio pictures, there's nothing stopping anyone from directing a short. The resulting diversity is one of the reasons why the most exciting ideas and groundbreaking work are in short films. In fact, it even works to your advantage if you are not a heterosexual white male because there are countless film festivals around the world which champion films by women, Asians, gays, etc.

So who makes short films? Everyone!

• *BIG NAME DIRECTORS*

We're not talking about the short films made by directors back when they were in film school, like Spike Lee's 1983 NYU film, *Joe's Bed-Stuy Barbershop: We Cut Heads*, or George Lucas' 1967 USC piece, *Electronic Labyrinth: THX 1138 4EB*. We're talking already established directors tackling the short format, such as the distinguished gentlemen who attempted the Lumière anniversary project. Or John Woo, Ang Lee, Tony Scott, John Frankenheimer, and Guy Ritchie making sponsored five-minute-long movies for the BMW web site.

If you are in this league, the rest of us salute you for bringing attention to the short format. People who have never seen a short film before will be exposed to one via your work. If they enjoyed yours, perhaps they'll want to check out more by other filmmakers. So thanks for reminding the world that shorts are an art form worthy of your time and effort. You might, however, not enjoy the experience of making a short film. Many feature film directors discover that it's easier to do a good job on a big studio picture because you have the money, resources, and screen time to make it work. With a short, screen time is so limited that to construct a complete story requires a completely different filmmaking skill. Comparisons to writing a short story versus a novel (or running a hundred-yard dash versus a marathon) apply.

Why don't more big name directors tackle the short form? They do, all the time, by making commercials. Remember the stylish black-and-white Gap ad depicting Christina Ricci and Dennis Hopper playing chess? Directed by the Coen Brothers! Spike Lee and Spike Jonze have also made many commercials that are basically short films. A-list directors have so little free time, why should they waste it making art on their own dime when they can get paid to do very expensive art pieces for others?

• MOVIE STARS

Bet you didn't know that Sandra Bullock wrote and directed a 1998 short film starring herself and Matthew McConaughey. It's called *Making Sandwiches*, and it played at Sundance. In 1995, Christine Lahti won an Oscar for a short she directed called *Lieberman in Love*. Ethan Hawke's 1994 black-and-white short, *Straight to One*, was filmed in the Chelsea Hotel, where he would later set his 2001 feature, *Chelsea Walls*. Other actors who frequently make shorts include *The Sweet Hereafter* actress Sarah Polley and *Six Feet Under*'s Rachel Griffiths. We commend any star who is willing to going out on a limb and make a short when they could just as easily spend their precious spare time cheering on the Lakers. Right, Jack?

• INDUSTRY PROFESSIONALS

Everyone wants to direct, but it's hard to break free from the industry perception of you. When choreographer Adam Shankman decided to make the transition, studio executives must have scoffed, "He's just a dancer. How do we know he can direct?" Shankman proved it in 1998 by creating a slick twenty-minute short called *Cosmo's Tale.* Now he's directing big studio pictures starring Jennifer Lopez (*The Wedding Planner*) and Steve Martin (*Bringing Down the House*).

If you're a working professional, you have the advantage of invaluable connections and favors you can call in. Don't save them up for later. If you want to make the transition, now's the time to capitalize on all the good will you've built up over the years. Remember, your colleagues and vendors want you to succeed so that you can hire them when you're directing Jennifer Lopez features. They want to help you join the big leagues. Let them.

•*REGULAR PEOPLE WITH NO INDUSTRY CONNECTIONS*

The actual number of established directors, actors, or industry professionals making shorts is very small. The majority of people picking up a camera are regular everyday people with a burning passion to make a film. Don't think just because you live in Nebraska and don't know anyone in Hollywood that you can't make a successful short film. If you review the list of filmmakers who get their shorts into the Sundance Film Festival, you'll be amazed by how many of them you've never heard of. Because they're just regular people with no Hollywood connections. People just like you. Why not join the ranks?

•*STUDENTS*

Of course, students still make up a large percentage of the short filmmaking population. University of Southern California School of Cinema Television graduate David Birdsell points out, "It's tough to break into filmmaking, to just decide 'I'm going to be a filmmaker!' If you go to film school, you immediately are in this little community of aspiring filmmakers. You have access to your fellow students and the equipment. You're also learning from each other and helping each other on projects. So it's not as lonely and daunting a prospect." In this new era when one can buy all the necessary filmmaking tools for the cost of one semester's tuition, is it really worth being a student filmmaker? We'll cover the pros and cons of film school in more detail in Chapter 4.

THE MAJOR STUMBLING BLOCK

If it's so easy to make a film and anyone can do it, why aren't millions of shorts being made every year? The easy answer is money. Movie-making at all levels — from the most guerilla indie shoots to the most bloated Hollywood blockbusters — costs money. Although you will learn as you make your way through this book that the short filmmaker's mantra must be "Everything for Free!", the inescapable fact remains that it does honestly cost a considerable amount of money to make and market a successful short film.

The good news is it doesn't take as much as it takes to make and market a feature. The old budgetary figure people used to throw around is $1,000 a minute to make a short film. So if you wanted to make a five-minute short film, you have to come up with $5,000. In the new era of desktop filmmaking, anything goes. The thing to keep in mind is that you can easily spend $20,000 on a short, but unless you sell it to HBO and Canal+, you probably won't get your money back.

In reality, how much money you need to make a short depends on (a) the nature of your project, (b) how much you can get for free, and (c) how much you are willing to spend. If you can get away with it, don't spend anything. Beg, borrow, and steal. Cash in every favor owed. Barter services. Do anything you can do to make your film, yet not end up massively in debt.

However, make no mistake: Filmmaking is an expensive venture. No matter how little you plan on spending to make your short, you will still need some cash in hand. So how do you get funding? It's easy.

GET MONEY FROM OTHER SOURCES

The first rule of filmmaking is don't spend your own money. Correction, that's the first rule of feature filmmaking. In short filmmaking, the director is usually bankrolling the project.

There are companies that will give you money to make a short film. Because these opportunities come and go, do a Google search under "short film funding" to see what's currently available. For a while, dot-com companies like AtomShockwave were paying filmmakers to make sponsored films for car companies like Ford (and of course BMW paid those big name directors to do flicks for their *www.bmwfilms.com* web site). Quite frankly, who among us doesn't want a car company throwing money at us to make a film? If you can get such a gig, great! However, you must remember this paid-for piece will not reflect your personal vision; it will be a glorified commercial, with the money people's input overriding your creative voice. Still, it's somebody else paying you to direct, and isn't that what we all dream of?

If you discover a company currently funding shorts, your mindset should be, "They're going to give that money to someone, why shouldn't it be me?!" So go ahead and apply, but don't sit around waiting for that money to land in your lap. Spending time researching sponsored programs and grants and then filling out the required paperwork can be an excuse not to cross the aspiring filmmaker/actual filmmaker bridge. So by all means, apply for funding (free money is the ultimate "Everything for Free!" item), but also come up with a way that you can make the film you want to make on the money you yourself can raise. Maybe you need to put aside your big expensive sponsor-worthy idea and make a more modest alternative project while waiting for that big money ship to come in.

SPEND YOUR OWN MONEY

Realistically, you're probably going to fund your short yourself. It's time to look at your bank account or credit card limit and decide how much you can afford to spend right here, right now. Is it $20,000? $2,000? $200? $20? If it's in the higher region, you can be more ambitious (shoot on film, shoot for several days, feed extras, etc.). However, even if it's $20, that's not going to stop you from making a film! With a $20 budget, your short might not be the grand opus you thought you were going to make, but you can still afford to run a tape through a borrowed mini-DV camera. You can still be a short filmmaker.

TEN EASY WAYS TO RAISE A LITTLE BIT OF CASH

Say you need more than twenty bucks. How can you get your hands on a little more dough?

1

GARAGE SALE

Time to turn purchases back into hard currency. Pick a good weekend to hold a garage sale, then ask your friends, family, neighbors, and co-workers to contribute their old junk. Before you put their things out for sale, go through the donations. Any good props or wardrobe you can use in your film? Anything that might fetch a better price on eBay?

2
EBAY

Sometimes junk that will go for $2.50 at a garage sale can be auctioned off for $25.00 on eBay. Why not give it a shot?

3
RENT PARTY

Think of it as a modest charity fundraiser. Or a house party with a cover charge. These parties have an additional benefit of being good networking opportunities. With friends bringing friends, who knows who will be hanging out in your kitchen? A musician whom you can talk into scoring your film? An artist who will help with set decoration? An actress who might be perfect for your lead? You never know! By the way, speaking of house parties, the feature film *House Party* was based on a short film. Bodes well for you, don't you think?

4
BENEFIT CONCERT

Ask the musicians who are going to do your film score to play the local bar as a fundraiser. It's certainly a lot less work for you than holding a garage sale or a rent party. And more fun, too.

5
FREE HAIRCUT DAY

Get inspired by Spike Lee's student film, *Joe's Bed-Stuy Barbershop: We Cut Heads.* The same benevolent hair and make-up artist who is going to volunteer to work on your film for free might be convinced to do a haircut marathon. The trick is to do men's hair only — much faster! With a suggested donation of $20 per head, those Andrew Jacksons can really add up.

6
SPONSORED STUNT

You know how you're always getting asked to sponsor someone's walkathon? It's payback time — their turn to sponsor you. You can do your own version of a walkathon, or you can do something more outrageous. It can be as silly as asking people to pay a certain amount per body you cram into a VW bug at the local Volkswagen dealership. Additionally, a stunt can be a priceless opportunity to get media attention. Let the local newspapers and television news stations know about your crazy event. Not only will local coverage give you something to put in your press kit, you never know what other opportunities might arise from having your community know about your project. Certainly it will be easier to ask favors later on when people have already heard about you and the outrageous things you'll do to become a filmmaker.

7
BAKE SALE/LEMONADE STAND

Little kids undercharge for their products! You can easily overcharge for your homemade food and drinks if you conduct your business in the right setting. What about the break room at work?

8
CAR WASH

Another idea stolen from those rank amateur kids. How are you going to compete with earnest middle school students trying to raise money for new football team uniforms? Well, you know those pretty actresses you're going to hire to be in your film? Talk 'em into helping out.

9
SELL YOUR BLOOD/SPERM

You won't even notice it's missing.

10
SELL YOUR DVD/CD COLLECTION

It's a tough bullet to bite, but you need the cash. You can always buy them again when you're rich. And, really, how many times do you need to watch *Reservoir Dogs* anyway?

MAKE AN "IN THE CAN" CONTRACT WITH YOURSELF

So how much money do you really need to make a short? This is where you have to change your way of thinking. Instead of thinking how much money you need, you need to think of how much you honestly can earmark for filmmaking at this moment in time. Write that number down. Seal it in an envelope. Don't let anyone else know this magic number. Promise yourself you will not spend more than this number during production. No matter what!

What you have done by sealing that envelope is you've made a contract with yourself to spend not a dime more than that amount getting your film "in the can." By "in the can," I mean you have enough money to buy film (or tape), run it through the camera during production, and get the exposed film back into the can (or tape cassette box). Your next step is to move into postproduction (i.e., get the film out of the can). If you have enough money in that initial funding to get you through post and marketing, you're all set! If not, you'll have to raise more money. Time for another visit to the blood bank!

The good news is, unlike production, there's no real time crunch in post. Postproduction can take years (don't worry, yours won't). More good news: There are more opportunities to beg for free services in post and practically no people to feed (that's where the money goes in production). Plus, you'll be motivated by the experience of actually having shot your film. If you need to get a second job to raise the money, you'll do it. Or better yet, start right now sticking a little something away from each paycheck for your post budget. Don't forget that you'll need even more money for marketing. Some filmmakers advise setting aside at least $1,000 for playing the festival circuit. But let's not get ahead of ourselves.

You want to make a short film. With your envelope money, you now have the funds to make one. It may not be the grand epic you originally dreamed of, but you have enough money to make something. Congratulations!

SHORT RECAP

• No one can stop you from becoming a filmmaker.

• Making a short is something to be proud of. Just ask Jack Nicholson.

- If you can find a company giving away money to make shorts, take the money! But most likely you'll finance your project yourself.

- It may be hard to raise a lot of money, but it's not hard to raise a little.

- You don't have to raise your entire budget at once. Just set aside enough cash to get you through production.

CHAPTER 2

FIRST, WATCH SOME FILMS

Many strange and wonderful things can happen in a very short time.

Too many filmmakers cling to the outdated idea that to be successful they have to make a short that could be mistaken for a feature film. In their minds, that means thirty minutes or longer, with studio-

quality production value. Certainly, amazing work has been done in the thirty- to fifty-minute range. But it's wrong to assume a "good" film has to be a mini-feature. Not only are half-hour pieces financially daunting, they aren't necessarily the best use of the format. Before you begin thinking about making your own masterpiece, do yourself a favor and check out what other filmmakers have done with the genre. You'll discover that with a little innovation and a lot of creativity, one can make a film that will blow everyone away, and it doesn't have to be more than a few minutes long.

WHAT DEFINES A SHORT

Because shorts can incorporate so many different kinds of filmmaking (narrative, experimental, live action, animation, documentary, mixed media, etc.), the best way to define a short is by running time. The Academy of Motion Picture Arts & Sciences classifies a short film as forty minutes and under. A now-defunct Internet company called MediaTrip declared anything under sixty minutes a short. The still-functioning AtomShockwave draws the line at forty. The Independent Film Channel wants films no longer than half an hour. For the Sundance Film Festival, fictional shorts must have a running time of less than seventy minutes while a doc has to clock in under fifty (however, to be eligible for competition, thirty-five minutes is the cutoff for both genres). As for the Sundance Online Film Festival, twenty minutes is the limit.

Practically speaking, anything over thirty minutes is on the long side. Those films are sometimes jokingly called "mediums." For festivals, online exhibition, and potential theatrical distribution, shorter is definitely better.

SHORTS SHOULD BE SHORT, SHOULDN'T THEY?

Ask any festival programmer, sales agent, or acquisition executive, and they will tell you that most shorts are too long. Thomas Harris, who programmed the Los Angeles Film Festival and the Palm Springs International Festival of Short Films, remarks, "When a short goes over fifteen minutes, you watch the film thinking, 'This could be shorter. What could be edited out?'"

Amy Talkington, who has written and directed five short films to date, admits, "My first film was eighteen minutes long. It was an example of a feature story trying to fit in a short film. My last film was nine minutes, and that feels like a good length. Stories can be told in fifteen minutes or less — and should be. Just being practical, the festival environment really doesn't allow for films over fifteen, at least not very much."

"Think about it," festival circuit veteran George Langworthy chimes in. "If you're a festival programmer and you have a film that's thirty minutes long, you can play three to six other shorts in the time taken up by this long one. So the longer film often gets knocked out. Personally, I think a half-hour short is awesome. But it's difficult to play festivals. If you make a one-minute-long film and it's good, chances are very good that it's going to play everywhere — because programmers always have an extra minute! However, you can't really do much in a minute. I'd say the great shorts are generally around twelve to fifteen minutes."

Knowing that shorter is better for festivals, some filmmakers resort to shaving off credit time when reporting their length. For example, when asked the running time of his film *White Face*, Brian McDonald replies, "It's twelve minutes. With the credits, it's a little over fourteen minutes." *Deveria* director Mat Fuller also plays that game. "I started telling my movie length minus the credits just to get it in festivals," Fuller confesses. "I say twenty, but it's really twenty-two."

Shorter is also better for television sales. "I get a lot of filmmakers who assume they should make a twenty-two minute film because of the half-hour television slot," declares distributor David Russell, whose Burbank-based company, Big Film Shorts, has been in business since 1996. "But nobody's buying independently produced short films to fill half-hour slots. Shorts are used as filler and interstitials in most cases. To make your film thinking that's the perfect length to sell to TV, that's just wrong. With those novella lengths, you're not going to get theatrical exhibition or be played on television as filler. However, with video-on-demand and DVD collections, there is some room for longer lengths in the marketplace."

Megan O'Neill, director of acquisitions for San Francisco-based AtomShockwave, adds, "Longer is always tougher. The longer you make your short, the higher the bar you've set for yourself. It has to be phenom-enal, like Peter Sollett's *Five Feet High and Rising*, which is twenty-nine minutes but won all sorts of awards. It has to be such a great short that people will go out of their way to program it. A festival or a television pro-grammer, an online or a DVD acquisition executive, somebody is going to have to say, 'This film is so good that we need to give it to our audience, no matter what!' In ten years of doing this, I can probably name on two hands how many longer films that have had that kind of success. Once you go over thirty minutes, it's almost impossible. *Decade of Love* is the only American one I can think of. Longer is definitely a harder sell. You better get an Academy Award nomination. You better be a festival darling. Otherwise, fifteen minutes and under is always better for sales."

SEE FOR YOURSELF

Most people want to make a long film because that's what they think a short film is. If they only saw the wide range of things accomplished in fif-teen minutes or less, they'd have a whole new mindset.

To check out what filmmakers are doing right now, go to film festivals or short film showcases. You'll discover that festivals do play films of all lengths. But you'll also note that the longer films are ghettoized in short film programs. The fifteen-minutes-or-less films get to play with the big boys in prime time, opening for the premieres and in front of the competition films.

You can also see shorts in the privacy of your own home if your cable or satellite service offers the Independent Film Channel or the Sundance Channel. Naturally, if you're trying to save money to make your own film, you shouldn't be squandering large amounts of cash every month on an outrageous cable bill! But for research purposes, you might want to order the indie channels for a little while. If you're going to sample the Sundance Channel, do it in December, when they devote a special day to playing shorts around-the-clock. Which day? December 21, the shortest day of the year! During the rest of the year, both Sundance and IFC have dedicated times in which short films are grouped together and used as regular programming. And when they need to fill time between features with "interstitial" programming, they'll throw on a short. You'll see shorts used as interstitial programming on HBO/Cinemax and STARS/Encore as well.

Up until recently, cable channels (and PBS) were the only place to see shorts if you didn't go to festivals. Now there's the World Wide Web, where short films flourish. It's estimated that there are over 10,000 shorts on the web. When it comes to viewing films on the Internet, you'll discover that it's a much more enjoyable experience if you have high-speed access. If you don't have it at home, go to the local library and use their computers. It's worth the effort rather than suffering with a slow delivery. A good place to begin your viewing is *www.ifilm.com* or *www.atomfilms.com*.

Don't forget home video. Student and early work by David Lynch, Jane Campion, Tim Burton, George Lucas, and Robert Rodriguez are all available either on DVD compilations of short films or as bonus material on features.

Lastly, many museums and libraries have film collections that you can view with special arrangements. If you are ever in Los Angeles, you can arrange with the Academy of Motion Picture Arts & Sciences to view video copies of any of the nominated and winning short films in their library. It's quite an eye-opening experience.

Many things will happen as you begin to view a wide variety of films. You'll see terrible shorts, which will serve to inspire you in an "I can do much better than that!" kind of way. You'll also see some amazing pieces that will inspire you to want to make something equally as great. On the downside, you might get depressed when you realize that there are filmmakers out there who have access to more money and better resources than you do. How can you expect to compete? Easy answer: by making something unique. Remember, everyone sees top-of-the-line filmmaking every day in feature films and on television. No one expects your little short to be in that league. What viewers want to see is the unexpectedly wonderful and weird stuff that they can only see in shorts. "What I like best about short films is the world that they take me to," remarks Sundance Film Festival programmer Trevor Groth. "People take chances with shorts that they can't do with features. You'll see stuff that you couldn't imagine, that you never thought you'd see on film, and there it is!"

EIGHT MILLION STORIES IN THE NAKED CITY

If you watch a lot of films, you might discover that your great idea for a short has already been done. Take, for example, *The Lunch Date*. Filmmaker Adam Davidson was still a student at Columbia in the late 1980s when he made this eleven-minute piece, shot in black and white at Grand Central Station. The story focuses on an elderly suburban woman who comes into the city to shop and misses her train back. With extra time on her hands but very little cash, she orders a salad from one of the food establishments in the train terminal. She sets her shopping bags and salad down at a table, then realizes she's forgotten to get a fork. When she returns to her table, there is a homeless man sitting there, eating her salad. She doesn't know what to do. She's hungry, has no money to buy another salad, and doesn't want to be intimidated by the homeless man. So she picks up her fork and begins eating the salad as well. The homeless man gives her a look, but continues to eat her salad. There's a nice moment when he gets up and returns with two cups of coffee, which he shares with her. But they never speak.

Her train is announced, and the woman gets up to leave. She's halfway down the track when she realizes she forgot her shopping bags back at the food stand. She rushes back, to discover her uneaten salad on the table with her shopping bags. She laughs as she realizes she mistook the homeless man's salad for her own. *The Lunch Date* is a wonderful, pitch-perfect film which was awarded the student Academy Award, the Palme d'Or at Cannes, and the 1990 Oscar for best live action short.

Every so often there's another version of a *Lunch Date*-like encounter showing up on the festival circuit. Once it was a stuffy British businessman at a London train station thinking another businessman had stolen his packet of potato chips, only to discover his had fallen to the ground. Another was a guy on a subway accusing another man of stealing his watch, only to discover later he left his watch at home. It's a situation that works in many variations.

An Occurrence at Owl Creek Bridge is another story told and retold. The 1962 original, directed by Robert Enrico and based on an Ambrose Bierce story, begins with a Civil War-era soldier being hung. At the moment the rope is about to snap his neck, the rope breaks and the man escapes. He runs home, where his wife is waiting to greet him, only to be jerked out of that fantasy when the hanging really does take place. In the 1998 Fox Movie Channel short, *Hope Street*, filmmaker Alex Metcalf set the story in modern day Los Angeles during a carjacking. Another short used a mountain climbing accident as the trigger. You can probably come up with your own version right now. It's not wrong to do your own twist on this classic tale, which clearly works well in the short format. You should just be aware that it's been done before.

TEN MUST-SEE SHORT FILMS

As you join the short filmmaking ranks, you will see countless short films of varying quality. To start you off with a solid sampling, here are ten films that will spur your creativity and make you realize how much can be accomplished in a very short time.

1

PEEL

Filmmaker: Jane Campion
Year: 1982
Running Time: 9 minutes

Peel is arguably the most perfect narrative short ever made under ten minutes. Although many people are

fans of Jane Campion's *Passionless Moments*, the greatness of her first film (a Palme d'Or winner) cannot be denied. Set during a family outing, the film is about a little boy who throws orange peels out the car window and the driver who wants him to stop. "It is so profound," raves fan George Langworthy. "It brings to the fore some of the most profound issues about family, parenthood, childhood, love, and stubbornness. It goes into this very sublime moment toward the climax. It's filled with suspense, and it's funny! It's an amazing film." Even two decades later, *Peel* is still being revived and shown in theaters around the world. You can see it on the Women Make Movies video compilation, *The Films of Jane Campion*.

2

MORE

Filmmaker: Mark Osborne
Year: 1999
Running time: 6 minutes

The perfect no-dialogue short is a six-minute claymation masterpiece about an elderly corporate drone working on a secret project that could bring bliss to the world. The film won the 1999 Sundance Film Festival and was nominated for an Academy Award. It's also the first stop-motion animated short originated for 70mm/15perf projection or Giant Screen format (IMAX). Filmmaker Mark Osborne explains, "Oddly, when I initially made *More*, it was just an attempt to make a spec music video. It turned into something much bigger, of course. But it was inspired by the music, the New Order song, and it represents the type of music video that I love and would want to do. It cost about $120,000 total to make. People think that's expensive for a short, but if you look at it as an IMAX film that was done independently, if it weren't for all the donated services, we would have spent half a million on it." The film's sales agent, Carol Crowe of Los Angeles-based Apollo Cinema, adds, "There's been such a huge continued interest in this film. I think even Mark Osborne would tell you he's surprised it keeps going. Why is it so popular? I think the subject matter is timely with everything going on with corporate America today. It has no dialogue, but it has a strong message. It's also a beautiful film. And the music is incredible, too." *More* is available via the filmmaker's web site *www.happyproduct.com*.

3
UN CHIEN ANDALOU
Filmmaker: Luis Buñuel (with Salvador Dali)
Year: 1928
Running time: 17 minutes

This extremely weird silent film was shot in two weeks with money supplied by the filmmaker's mother. The highly experimental piece was a collaboration between Luis Buñuel and Salvador Dali, two relatively unknown artists who wanted to make something that would shock audiences — and call a little attention to themselves. Decades later we're still disturbed by the imagery, including the infamous razor blade to the eyeball. When *Entertainment Weekly* ran a 2003 cover story ranking the Top Fifty Cult Movies of all time, *Un Chien Andalou* came in at twenty-two (between *Pee-Wee's Big Adventure* and *Akira*). Order a video copy of this film on Amazon to be inspired to make a calling card film that will not only achieve your immediate goals but continue to amaze viewers half a century later. A tall order, indeed. It helps, of course, if you're as talented as Buñuel and Dali.

4
POWERS OF TEN
Filmmakers: Charles and Ray Eames
Year: 1977
Running time: 9 minutes

This film by acclaimed artists Charles and Ray Eames takes only eight minutes and forty-seven seconds to document how a molecule on a man resting on a picnic blanket in a grass field in Florida relates to the farthest extremes of the universe. With constant play in schools and institutions, *Powers of Ten* is probably one of the most viewed short films of the modern era. We should all be so gifted to create a film that is just as elegant, informative, and impressive as it was when the artists completed it a quarter century ago. Available on the DVD collection *Eames Video, Volume 1*.

5
LE JETÉE
Filmmaker: Chris Marker
Year: 1962
Running time: 29 minutes

Another oldie but goodie that will blow your mind. Made in 1962 by photographer/filmmaker Chris Marker, this French film feels more complete than the 1996 Brad Pitt/Bruce Willis feature-length adaptation, *12 Monkeys.* What's amazing about this very experimental yet mesmerizing time travel tale is that the entire film consists of still photographic images (with one short section of moving pictures). A filmmaker couldn't pull that off for ninety minutes, but for half an hour it gives viewers a movie-watching experience they'll never forget. You own a digital still camera, you have the computer software — go out and make your own *Le Jetée*-inspired piece. But make it fifteen minutes or less! *Le Jetée* is available on VHS and DVD.

6

THE OPERATION

Filmmaker: Jacob Pander
Year: 1995
Running Time: 16 minutes

A new take on an old genre, *The Operation* is a radioactive sex film. Jacob Pander shot his highly erotic short with an infrared video camera. Set in an operating room, the action revolves around a graphic sexual encounter between a surgeon and her patient. Shot over two days with a crew of five people, the indie flick won an award at the 1995 Chicago Underground Film Festival. Fan Joel S. Bachar raves, "If you strip it down, it's a porn. But it's shot with one of those infrared cameras that the military uses to look for people in bunkers. So everything that is hot (you can imagine) comes off super hot, and everything that's dark (like cartilage and eyes) is dark. So these people look like alabaster translucent aliens having sex. Really brilliant film!" Available where fine pornography is sold — on the Internet (search under the director's name and the film title).

7

HARDWARE WARS

Filmmaker: Ernie Fosselius
Year: 1977
Running time: 13 minutes

If you want to make a short film that people will clamor to see (and it's not about sex!), make a *Star Wars* parody. Thanks to George Lucas' tolerance, there's a whole slew of *Star Wars*-inspired shorts (in fact, there's an entire category on *www.atomfilms.com* devoted to them). As you might expect, the first entree into the genre took place shortly after the original *Star Wars* was released. Ernie Fosselius wrote and directed an intentionally super cheesy and very funny flick that has a devoted following to this day. How to explain *Hardware Wars'* continued popularity? "Filmmakers enjoy the joke (and see the potential for their own work) of making something look 'big' with cheesy effects, sets and costumes," surmises producer Michael Wiese. "They are inspired by the insight that they can parody their favorite films, characters, and TV shows. I even heard during a film festival panel as career strategy proposal that 'you can get rich and famous by making a parody of *Star Wars!*' For me, I like that we made something for nothing and it worked." *Hardware Wars* is now available on a special collector's edition DVD through *www.mwp.com*. The magic of *Star Wars* parody worked again in 1999 when Joe Nussbaum retold *Shakespeare in Love*, substituting USC film school student George Lucas as the hero struggling for inspiration. Unlike its pred-ecessor, *George Lucas in Love* is not a cheap film. High production value, a strong story, good acting, and a rich score make it heads and shoulders above the average *Star Wars* parody. In fact, when *George Lucas in Love* was first released on home video, it sold more copies on Amazon than Lucas's most recent *Star Wars* installment. Both VHS and DVD versions of *George Lucas in Love* continue to rack up impressive sales on Amazon.

8

SUPERSTAR: THE KAREN CARPENTER STORY
Filmmaker: Todd Haynes
Year: 1987
Running time: 45 minutes

When Todd Haynes decided to tell the life story of anorexic pop singer Karen Carpenter, he had a brilliant no-budget take: instead of actors, he'd do it with dolls. Great idea, yes? Not according to Mattel (Barbie's manufacturer), or Karen's brother, who controls the rights to the Carpenters' music and who wasn't portrayed very nicely in the film. *Superstar* is probably the most famous short film that can't be distributed due to legal issues. The notoriety (and the fact that the film is pretty great) made director Todd Haynes' career. Although it's not supposed to be commercially available, you might be able to find illegal copies of *Superstar* on the Internet.

9
405
Filmmakers: Bruce Branit and Jeremy Hunt
Year: 2000
Running time: 4 minutes

The IFILM Internet Movie Guide ranks *405* as the best short film on the web. It's one of the most popular Internet films ever, with over 4.5 million views to date. The story involving a jet, a little old lady, and a busy Los Angeles freeway took only one weekend to shoot with a single chip DV camera (the Canon Optura). Even the extensive CGI didn't take long — just three-and-a-half months of directors Bruce Branit and Jeremy Hunt working after hours and on weekends while holding down day jobs. *405* is so impressively done that the filmmakers were immediately snapped up by hot shot talent agency CAA. Although VHS copies are for sale, most people see *405* on *www.ifilm.com*.

10
SPIRIT OF CHRISTMAS
Filmmakers: Trey Parker and Matt Stone
Year: 1995
Running time: 5 minutes

Definitely the most financially and culturally successful short film ever made, *Spirit of Christmas* is a five-minute jewel that launched the *South Park* empire. When Fox executive Brian Graden gave Trey Parker and Matt Stone two thousand dollars to make a video Christmas card, little did he know a pop cultural phenomenon would spring from their crudely animated story of four foul-mouthed kids who have to pick sides when Santa and Jesus have a showdown at the local mall. Although the filmmakers didn't plan it, the short is a de facto pilot for the series, establishing everything from the South Park location to the "killed Kenny" catch phrase.

Here's to hoping that your short will be as creatively outrageous and outrageously profitable as *Spirit of Christmas*!

SHORT RECAP

- Shorts can be any length — but fifteen minutes or less is ideal.

- Longer films are harder to get into festivals and on television. Why invest all that time and money if no one will see it?

- If your "original idea" has been done before, make sure you have a good twist — and that yours is better than your predecessors.

- Shorts are the perfect venue for trying out different filmmaking techniques. Experiment!

- Make a short that people will still want to watch decades after you made it. That's the true definition of a successful short.

CHAPTER 3

THINK LIKE A SHORT FILMMAKER

Remember, you're not making a feature!

Feature filmmakers have to play by the rules. They are creating very expensive works of art that have potentially great commercial value. Short filmmakers aren't. Therefore, we don't have to play by any rules. This is why

short filmmaking is artistically more fulfilling than feature filmmaking.

Too many people approach short filmmaking with a feature mentality. Those are the people who blow $75,000 on a thirty-minute film that no one wants to see. Meanwhile, scrappy DV filmmaker Brian McDonald spends $1,000 on a fourteen-minute mocumentary called *White Face*, which wins the audience award at Slamdance, sells to HBO, gets picked up by a diversity training company, and ultimately nets him $100,000. Which path do you want to follow?

If you want to make a short film for practically no money, you don't have to sacrifice production value. You just need to think differently.

YOU ARE NOT MAKING A FEATURE — YOU ARE MAKING A SHORT!

Always remind yourself that you're not making *Gone with the Wind*. No one expects your little film to be the next great cinematic masterpiece that will change the face of filmmaking forever. It's just a short film. So relax and have fun.

"It's the truest form of filmmaking that exists," declares Carol Crowe, President of Los Angeles-based short film distribution company Apollo

Cinema. "You don't need big names, big wows, or special effects. You just need truly a good story. In fact, a good short is like a short story, it can stick in your memory and last."

Don't obsess about making *pretty* pictures that can match the multi-million dollar extravaganzas you see at the local multiplex. Obsess about making *moving* pictures. Moving, meaning there is motion on screen. Too many shorts are static: stationary camera, actors planted in one spot, and very little action taking place. You're not directing a play — or a soap opera! Moving, meaning the film is well paced. Unlike feature filmmakers, you don't have enough screen time to show mundane activities like walking somewhere, knocking on the door, waiting for it to be answered, then crossing over the threshold. After sitting through dozens of shorts while his own played the festival circuit, director Noah Edelson noticed how many began with someone walking somewhere. It got to the point where Noah wanted to yell at the ambling characters, "It's a short film! You should be there already!" Moving, meaning your film affects the viewer — makes them jump, laugh, cry, or close their eyes in fear. "The audience isn't expecting the same sort of formula as a feature film," explains filmmaker David Birdsell. "They're willing to go in a completely unknown direction. At the same time, you made a short film, and you had limited resources, right? It doesn't matter to the audience what your resources were. They just want to be entertained or enlightened or whatever." Short film viewers will forgive a variety of filmmaking flaws as long as they're enjoying the flick. "Audiences really get a kick out of seeing shorts that take chances that a lot of the features can't," points out Trevor Groth, programmer of the Sundance Film Festival. "Over the eleven years that I've been doing this, the short programs at Sundance have been the highest attended of any of the sections of the festival."

Unlike feature filmmaking, there are no rules in short filmmaking. Anything and everything can happen in a short. "I had fun doing a piece where I made silicone molds of feet, hands, and a head," shares animator Eileen O'Meara. "Then I poured colored candle wax into the molds. I took the detailed and brightly colored body parts, melted them frame by frame with a blowtorch, and shot it backwards. The result was a sort of creation myth piece where humans form from a pool of wax. When I started the project, I realized I had to figure out how to make realistic wax body parts.

I found the guy that made statues for the Hollywood Wax Museum. He had trained at Madame Tussaud's and generously showed me the technique from beginning to end. It was great. The good thing about making a short is that if you do everything yourself and you fund it through your day job, you're not going to have an executive breathing down your neck telling you what to do. You get to make your own film and have complete control over it. The only problem is if it's not any good, you can't blame anyone else."

Allow yourself to run amok creatively. Go outside your comfort zone. Learn how to do amazing new things. Push the envelope. Don't play it safe. Come up with outrageous story ideas. Encourage your actors to take chances. Try some wacky tricks in post. Have fun with your titles and credits. Why not? After all, you're not making *Gone with the Wind*.

"Most people they do a few shorts, then for the rest of their life they concentrate on feature length films," sighs *Coven* director Mark Borchardt. "Features are a whole new universe — a whole new spectrum of money, a whole new spectrum of recognition. So these filmmakers kiss the short format goodbye. Whereas I'm interested in accommodating my personal ideology. If an idea calls for the length of a short film, I'll pursue that. But I think a lot of people, as soon as they make it, the idea of short film is over and out."

Filmmaker Karl Hirsch firmly believes you should not give up on shorts, even after you've graduated to features. "The best thing about short films is that they're fun to make, they're fun to watch, and it's a great inexpensive way to express yourself and to exercise the craft without going crazy and spending millions of dollars," exclaims Hirsch. "I've made a couple of features, and I have made several short films, none of which have cost over a thousand dollars. I've achieved more professionally, creatively, and emotionally from making those short films than I did doing features. Of course, I'm trying to make more features. But in the interim, it's a lot of fun to go on a set, shoot for a day with some actors — and have a blast."

Becoming a filmmaker isn't always fun in the sun. There's a big learning curve when you cross that bridge from wannabe filmmaker to actual filmmaker. Quite often we wish we could take Noah Edelson's advice and "be there already." The thing to remember is it doesn't have to be so hard. With the right mindset, it can be a blast. Let's aim for that!

THE TEN ESSENTIAL PRINCIPLES FOR SUCCESSFUL SHORT FILMMAKING

Before we go any further, let's review the ten golden rules for successful short filmmaking. Or rather, I used to call them golden rules — until I was reminded that there are no rules in short filmmaking. Consider these guiding principles, standard operating procedures, concepts, mantras, mottoes, whatever you want to call them. Knowing them will give you an unbeatable edge as you begin your short filmmaking career.

1

YOU ARE THE STUDIO.

When you're directing a feature film for Paramount, Paramount is the studio, and you are a person employed by Paramount to make a work for hire. Who finances the film? Paramount. Who has final creative control? Paramount. Who is in charge of marketing the film? Who gets to design the poster? Who is responsible for distributing the film? Who makes decisions regarding home video? Who profits from the film? Who gets sued if something goes wrong? Paramount, Paramount, Paramount, Paramount, Paramount, Paramount.

When you make a short, you are not only the person responsible for directing the film, you are also the studio. The answer to all of the above questions is you, you, you, you, you, you. Never again in your career will you have such an opportunity to handle every single part of the filmmaking process. It's exciting, educating, and very time consuming.

So, you are the studio. What kind of studio are you? Do you make big budget films or low budget films? Do you do all your paperwork properly and play by the rules, or are you a down-and-dirty, guerrilla-style production house? What are your capital assets? How much money do you want to spend on creating product? Do you expect to make any of this money back? What happens if someone does sue you, what will you do? These and many more questions must be answered.

You are the studio. As we go through the steps of production, know that each studio is unique. Make the decisions that work best for your studio. For example, for the shorts I produced for the Fox Movie Channel, I always paid for location permits. Didn't want to risk being shut down and felt it was worth the money. However, I know plenty of "studios" that risk it all the time. As a studio, I don't believe there are enough opportunities in terms of exhibition and distribution to produce a thirty-minute-long film. You as studio might only want to produce longer films — especially if you want to win an Academy Award (the Academy loves the longer films).

There's no wrong or right when you're the studio.

It's worth your while to really sit down and plan out a future for your studio. "If you're making shorts to get into features," counsels writer-director Amy Talkington, "make a film that is similar in tone and spirit to the feature you want to make. That is so incredibly important. I never stopped and said 'I want to do films about young people' — that's just what I did. I made several shorts about teenagers. So that's who I am. That's the kind of projects people bring to me. Because I'm making films about young people. And that's fine. But an intelligent person who is shaping her career might stop and think about it, and create a short similar in tone to her first feature script. That's a problem that I've had with a feature script that I've recently gone out with. They say 'Yeah, we see she's a great filmmaker, and it's a great script, but she hasn't made a film that really reflects this tone.' And I just want to strangle them! Because, look, you can see that I've nailed four or five different tones, why wouldn't I be able to nail this one?! But that's what they say. They really need to see it. So ideally that's what you go for."

Bergen Williams is an actress who took my UCLA Extension class and decided she was going to be a studio that made twelve DV shorts in a year — as learning experience. She went on eBay and bought a DV camera and Final Cut Pro. Knowing she was going to do a full year's worth of filming using SAG actors, she bought a year's worth of workers' compensation insurance. Thus armed, she officially opened her studio and went into business. And how did it turn out? Her first film landed her a writing gig on a television series! She made one other short, but I don't think she continued to do one a month. You could say her studio went out of business.

So, what kind of studio are you? The time to think about this is now — before we begin digging into the filmmaking process. This is your chance to do things the way you want. Your true character will be revealed. Don't want to do proper paperwork? Fine, you're the kind of studio that doesn't do paperwork. Don't want to clear your music? Fine, you're the kind of studio that is purely making art films and doesn't care about commercial exhibition. Don't want to feed your crew? Fine, you're the kind of studio no one wants to work for ever again.

Some people run their studio with an "I'm just a dumb short filmmaker, I don't know anything" mentality. Actually, I am a big proponent of this great excuse — it's true, you are just a dumb short filmmaker, you don't know anything, and sometimes it behooves you to take this easy out. Especially when you're getting busted for shooting without permits. But all the time? If your studio never interacts with professionals, then do whatever you want. It's when you ask others to take your studio seriously that you get in trouble. When you sign contracts, you're not just some dumb short film-maker with $20 in the bank — you are a studio that can be held account-able. People are expecting your studio to act just as professionally as the majors. The SAG rep who is dealing with you is also dealing with Paramount. If you expect the same consideration, you have to act just as a real studio does.

Think of it this way. As much as you'd like to think you're just messing around, you are building a property. When Mike Judge drew two moron heavy metal kids for his short *Frog Baseball*, he did not think he was creat-ing the Beavis and Butthead empire. Nor did Trey Parker and Matt Stone with *Spirit of Christmas*. Your little tiny film might result in something that can make your studio far richer than your grandest dreams. Take it seriously.

2
FILMMAKERS LIE.

Whether it's how long a scene is going to take to shoot or whether you liked what an actor is doing, you'll find yourself lying at every stage of the film-making process. Don't worry. It's part of your job. Know when you need to lie and when you need to be honest. And know that anyone who has ever dealt with a filmmaker knows filmmakers lie when they need to. So when people act like they don't believe you, they really don't.

The two organizations that you should never lie to because it will blackball your studio (and you) for the rest of your career are the Screen Actors Guild and the Academy of Motion Picture Arts & Sciences. When dealing with those two bodies, you don't mess around.

3

"EVERYTHING FOR FREE! EVERYONE WORKS FOR FREE!"

If you've got the money to make a short paying full rate for goods and services, go ahead and do so. Or stretch that amount out and make a feature. But most short film-makers are operating on a dime. If you're a "we have no money" studio, your working motto must be "Everything for Free! Everyone Works for Free!" This is not something you keep secret — you tell everyone. Write it in big letters, shout it from rooftops, tattoo it on your forehead: You are a studio that operates under the mandate "Everything for Free! Everyone Works for Free!"

You'll be surprised how many people are willing to work for free if they understand that no one is getting paid. It's only when people feel like they are being taken advantage of (or undervalued compared to others) that problems arise.

Always recite your list of freebies when asking for something else free: "Everyone's working for free. Panavision gave us a free camera, Kodak gave us free film, won't you give us free processing?" The more people and organizations who have waived their fees, the more others feel like they should jump on the bandwagon. Of course, Panavision might not have really given you a free camera by the time you're speaking to Kodak, and some crewmembers will not work without being paid. This is where you fall back on the previous motto: Filmmakers lie.

In general, you must remain constantly vigilant to your "Everything for Free!" modus operandi. Robert Rodriguez is your patron saint when it comes to this way of thinking. For *El Mariachi,* he refused to buy a can of black spray paint so they could paint the cover of a guitar case to match the hero guitar case. He found a way to shoot around the mismatched cover rather than paying a buck for a can of paint! As our patron saint says, once you start spending money, it's hard to stop. It becomes a dollar here, a dollar there, all of a sudden your budget goes out of control. Just refuse to spend money.

"Get out of Los Angeles or New York," advises bi-coastal filmmaker Amy Talkington. "Go to communities where people are more excited about a little movie. I made my two first shorts in Long Island, and found a lot of people were interested in donating free things. In both cases, we needed a picture car. We went to parking lots near our shooting locations and put flyers under the windshield wiper saying 'Do you want to be in pictures?' And we got cars for free in both instances."

That Strange Person director Eileen O'Meara discovered a downside of this modus operandi. "Once you start to get everything for free, your film's credits become frightfully long," O'Meara sighs. One way to solve this problem is having two versions of your film. One is the "thanks version" which only exists on tape and does indeed list everyone and their logos in large type. This version is given to everyone associated with the film. The other, "festival version" of your film, can have radically streamlined credits.

4

THINK ORGANICALLY.

If your studio is well financed, then you can be ambitious and plan on shooting anything anywhere. But if you're trying to stretch a buck, the best way to operate is think organically. Instead of adapting that Stephen King story you've always loved but will cost tens of thousands to do right, take a walk around your neighborhood, look around your bedroom, investigate what's up in your grandparents' attic, check out that classic Chevy Nova your sister's no-good boyfriend is so proud of. These are unique things which only you have access to — for free. Other filmmakers are wasting weeks leaving notes on the windshields of Novas all over this country, begging for free access. You can get one any time you want. What story can you tell using a Nova?

The universe has already lined up freebies for you if you would only open your eyes and look. Don't ask your volunteer art director to buy paints to alter a blank store window to read "Chicken For Sale" when a perfectly acceptable alternative might already be painted on the El Pollo restaurant two blocks from your house. You've got a home court advantage, use it!

5

IT'S JUST A MATTER OF GETTING THROUGH A NUMBER OF NOS UNTIL YOU HIT THAT ONE YES.

As you've discovered, the trick to getting things for free is just to ask for them. Sometimes you have to leave notes on one hundred cars before an owner will call you back and say yes. Sometimes the first person you approach will agree. When all this scrounging around gets you down, just remember there is a "yes" out there somewhere. What if you quit just five minutes before you come across it?

Why should people say yes to you? See #6.

6

YOU ARE A VERY TALENTED FILMMAKER WHO IS GOING TO GO FAR. PEOPLE ARE LUCKY TO BE WORKING WITH YOU.

This is the easiest principle of all to remember because you know it's true, but it doesn't hurt to remind yourself of it when you feel weird about begging. If Spielberg asked you to come work on his film for free, would you say yes? You're not Spielberg yet, but you might be. This is why people will say yes to you, too.

Remember, shorts are where the most exciting work is taking place. Most industry professionals wish they could work on projects they passionately believed in. They want you to be a genius. They want you to achieve your dream. They want to be on your team. They want to be nice guys. Give them the opportunity to do so. Go ahead. Ask.

Number One Fan director Amy Talkington is great at asking. "I really wanted my first short to look great and have a dark, moody feel," Talkington says. "There's a director of photography whose work I had admired, Jim Denault. He had shot Michael Almereyda's films and many other features.

[He's since done *Boys Don't Cry*.] I picked up the phone, dialed information — and he was listed! I called, he answered. I told him that I was a film student and had a script, that I knew he wasn't doing short films anymore, but would he take a look at it? He said, 'Sure, shove it under my door.' I did, he loved it, we met, he did the film for free. The lesson I learned is don't assume that someone doesn't want to do your project. If you have something that you're passionate about, and it's interesting, you'll be surprised what high levels of people are interested in coming along for the ride."

7

YOU WILL BE A PAYING CLIENT FOR THE REST OF YOUR CAREER. VENDORS WANT YOUR BUSINESS.

Just remind yourself of this when you approach vendors. It is why you will get free film, free cameras, free lights, free dollies, free processing, free telecine, free titles, etc. Kodak wants to get you while you're young and impressionable. That's why they give student discounts. Panavision wants you to know no other camera but theirs. That's why they will lend an inexperienced cinematographer extremely expensive equipment.

Why should a rental house do you a favor? Because you will give them loyalty for the rest of your career. Or so they hope. It's a buyer's market, even if you're not really buying right now. So go in to rental houses to investigate the equipment. Get free lessons. Ask to borrow that Hi-Def camera for the weekend so you can do some tests before committing to rent it for your four-week-long feature film shoot (lie). That's how free cameras are unofficially scored.

8

SHORTS REQUIRE LESS TIME INVESTMENT THAN FEATURES. THERE IS NO REAL FINANCIAL GAIN FOR ANYONE.

On your end, your goal should be to get in and out as quickly as possible. Don't procrastinate. Make a date to start shooting, then start shooting. Features wait forever to get a greenlight. You go now.

Short shoots are best. Features shoot for weeks on end. You can make an entire film in a weekend. In fact, weekends are the best time to shoot because that's when people and equipment are available.

Remember, those no-budget feature directors are trying to work the same angles you are. But in your case, you're asking for a much smaller favor. For example, the feature people need to borrow a free camera for four weeks — an entire month in which paying customers might be coming into the rental house, willing to lay down cash if only the vendor hadn't given away that camera for free. You're just asking a camera rental house (which would be closed for business over the weekend anyway) to take something off the shelf on Friday and reshelve it on Monday — with no financial loss to anyone. Which request do you think the rental house would be more willing to accommodate? Similarly, a big name art director has a week off between shows. She can squeeze your little project in, but she'll have to turn down the feature director who needs her for a month. If you stress how little time commitment you'll require, it will encourage people to say yes.

Not only are the feature people asking for bigger favors, they'll potentially make money off their project. Everyone knows there's no money in shorts. It's like poetry — it's still art for art's sake (although there are a few rare exceptions of those who can make a living at it). If a poet asked you to lend her a pen, wouldn't you feel benevolently inclined? If crew members or vendors ask for deferred compensation, you can dissuade them by explaining, "Deferrals makes sense with features, but with shorts there's no real financial gain for anyone."

Listen to yourself when you tell people there's no money in shorts. You're not lying. When you're tempted to start pouring more money than you planned into your film, stop and evaluate whether it's truly worth increasing your investment. Remember, there's no real financial gain for anyone!

9
NO STARS NECESSARY. YOU ARE THE STAR.

In feature filmmaking, if you have any hope of getting your film picked up for distribution, you better have recognizable names in the cast. With shorts, there is a certain amount of fuel behind a short that has a star involved, but it isn't necessarily a guarantee of success. Stars, in fact, distract from the short and make it feel more like television or a feature. In addition, you'll get less credit as a director. People won't say you made a great film, they'll exclaim, "That Jennifer Aniston short was great!" This is true also of star crewmembers. If you get Spielberg's director of photography [shorthand: DP], everyone will remark, "Of course that short is great, Spielberg's DP shot it!" However, don't let that stop you from going after names. Because they are gettable. And you will have an entirely different experience than you would if your best friend starred in it or shot it. Just remember it isn't necessary.

Megan O'Neill, director of acquisitions for the short film company AtomShockwave, adds, "I try to say this on every panel because it's really true. I've produced a feature, and with features you have a lot of other pressures on you — actors who want trailers, distributors who want the film to have a poster that looks like every other poster ever made, etc. With a short, you don't have any of that. This is your baby. You can really be an auteur on this film. So don't get hung up on stars. Make the best film you can. That's what's important."

10
SHORTS ARE
LEARNING
EXPERIENCES FOR
EVERYONE.

Festival programmers and short film distributors will tell you that they watch thousands of painfully amateurish disasters every year. Not that this is a surprise to anyone, because shorts are generally made by first-time directors trying to learn their craft. The proliferation of inexpensive digital cameras and editing systems means more people are giving filmmaking their best shot. Let's just say not everyone who dreams of growing up to be Martin Scorsese turns out to be as talented as Martin Scorsese.

The important thing to remember is that the world doesn't need another Martin Scorsese. That slot is already filled, thank you. So give yourself a break if your little DV boxing piece isn't quite up to *Raging Bull* standards. However, if your film really is a disaster, you as the studio can make the decision to shelve it. No need to admit the real reason that film is no longer on your release schedule. Lie and tell people that the lab ruined your negative, or the editing system ate your tape. Mark the disaster down as a learning experience and move on. But don't be too hasty. Most filmmakers cringe in horror when they go back to see their first effort. Even George Lucas, who still hasn't learned pacing, must think his student film is ungodly long (it is!). But that doesn't mean you and I aren't interested in seeing it (it's available on DVD). What if George put *Electronic Labyrinth: THX 1138 4EB* in the vault and never let anyone see it? Thankfully, Lucas knows (and we know) that shorts are a learning experience for everyone.

This rule, which applies to you as a filmmaker, also applies to everyone else involved in your project. If you're lucky and very connected, you might get Spielberg's DP to shoot your film. But more likely you'll get the camera assistant who pulls focus on Spielberg's second unit to be your DP. Everyone wants to move up the ranks, and one way to build up experience and credits is to work on shorts. Will this lowly camera operator make mistakes that a seasoned pro wouldn't? Yes. But before you kill him, remind yourself that shorts are a learning experience for everyone.

SHORT RECAP

- No-budget short filmmakers have it much easier than their feature equivalents.

- When you assume the role of a studio, you are responsible for everything. Do whatever you want, but take responsibility for your actions.

- One day you'll be Spielberg. Or rather, your own version of Spielberg.

- Give people the privilege of helping you achieve your dream.

- When things go wrong (and they will), avoid getting an ulcer by remembering that shorts are learning experience for everyone.

CHAPTER 4

ACT LIKE A FILMMAKER

You don't have to go to film school, but you do need to know how to do your job.

Enough with the theoretical. Let's get down to business. You would think the perfect way to become a filmmaker is to go to film school. After all, doctors have to go to med

school and lawyers to law school before they can practice. Shouldn't the same apply to filmmakers? In the old days, going to film school made a lot of sense because you had to get your hands on expensive and not very accessible filmmaking equipment to make movies. In this new era, anyone with a computer and a credit card can be a filmmaker. Why waste your money on tuition when you can better spend it buying an entire camera package and editing system on eBay?

Before we dismiss the idea of film school, let's give it the old pro and con rundown just to make sure we're making the right decision.

PROS OF GOING TO FILM SCHOOL

- Film school teaches you the basics of filmmaking.

- You learn from experts. Although street smarts, natural ability and the school of hard knocks have their good points, how much better is it to study at the feet of the masters? In the real world, mentors and gurus are harder to come by.

- You make mistakes in a no-risk environment. By the time your "official" film school project is unspooled in front of industry executives at a special screening organized and paid for by your school, you will have made countless unwatchable films that no one but your teachers and fellow students have seen. You don't have to be self-conscious about showing your peers these disasters because you know they're making equally bad monstrosities.

• You don't have to struggle to meet and hire crew members or actors. It's never easier to be an organic filmmaker than at film school.

• If you go to a prestigious film school, you'll have a solid entry point into Hollywood. Most of the major film schools around the country arrange annual Los Angeles premieres of their students' work, which Hollywood insiders take seriously. Industry bigwigs might not personally attend, but they'll send their assistant or request a screener tape. No one wants to miss out on the next Spielberg. Additionally, alumni are notoriously benevolent to new graduates. If you cold call former students and mention your connection, you'll get some meetings.

CONS OF GOING TO FILM SCHOOL

• You have to pay money for the privilege of learning. Why pay an institution when you can learn on your own? Take a page from the Kevin Smith playbook. He quit school and used his tuition money to make the feature film *Clerks*.

• You can't do whatever you want in terms of filmmaking. It's a structured environment.

• Although all you really want to do is direct, you'll have to take a variety of classes that have nothing to do with directing.

• Some schools own your work. Who owns George Lucas's student films? USC.

• You aren't necessarily guaranteed admission to the best schools. If you get stuck studying film in Nowheresville, will your degree mean anything in Hollywood? Probably not.

INSIDER ADVICE ON GOING TO FILM SCHOOL

"In film school, you get a chance to dabble with filmmaking, which you can do on your own, too, but film school can be a great place to do it," suggests

USC grad David Birdsell. "Doing a bunch of shorts very quickly — in our case, it was Super-8 — you get the hang of filmmaking and an inkling of your own sensibility and your own approach to filmmaking, which isn't necessarily a given. You don't just know automatically, 'Oh, I make this kind of film!' You try a few things while there's nothing at stake. You just dabble. Hopefully you know what you're doing by the end of that. Just like writing. You have to write some stuff to get a sense of your own voice."

Animator Eileen O'Meara is a perfect example of someone who found her filmmaking voice in school. "I did undergrad in fine art," O'Meara says. "Did a lot of photography, thought I was starting to repeat myself, and wanted to add the dimension of time. So I went to USC film school. When I was there doing live action, I took a side course of animation and realized that was the medium that fit my personality the most."

David Birdsell adds, "No one can teach you how to make a good film, but film school can teach you a lot of things that go into good film. Classes on screenwriting and cinematography are useful. But you can't really learn filmmaking without doing it. And film school provides an opportunity to do it on a small scale without a lot at stake. Other than tuition. Which, in my case at USC, was high."

Can't afford USC? Your local college probably offers more reasonably priced film-oriented classes you can take. The two filmmakers who made the Internet sensation *405* went to California State University of Long Beach (majoring in film production) and the University of Kansas (studying industrial design!).

TEN PLACES THAT WILL TEACH YOU HOW TO ACT LIKE A FILMMAKER

For those who want to follow in the footsteps of George Lucas (USC), Spike Lee (NYU), David Lynch (AFI), Tim Burton (Cal Arts) and even Jim Morrison of the Doors (UCLA), here is contact information for ten major American film schools (in alphabetical order):

1

AFI Conservatory
The American Film Institute

2021 North Western Avenue
Los Angeles, CA 90027
www.afi.com/education/conservatory/apply.asp
Tel: (323) 856-7600

2

Cal Arts
California Institute of the Arts
24700 McBean Parkway
Valencia, CA 91355-2397
www.calarts.edu
Tel: (661) 255-1050

3

Columbia University School of the Arts
Columbia University in the City of New York
305 Dodge Hall, Mail Code 1808
2960 Broadway
New York, NY 10027-6902
www.columbia.edu/cu/admissions
Tel: (212) 854-2875

4

Florida State University Film School
University Center 3100A
Tallahassee, FL 32306-2350
http://filmschool.fsu.edu/
Tel: (850) 644-7728

5

New York University Tisch School of the Arts
70 Washington Square South
New York, New York 10012
www.nyu.edu/tisch
Tel: (212) 998-1212

6

North Carolina School of the Arts
School of Filmmaking
1533 South Main Street
Winston-Salem, NC 27127
www.ncarts.edu
Tel: (336) 770-3290

7

Savannah College of Art and Design
Admission Department
P.O. Box 2072
Savannah, Georgia 31402-2072
www.scad.edu
Tel: (800) 869-7223

8

UCLA School of Theater, Film, and Television
University of California, Los Angeles
Department of Film and Television
Box 951622
Los Angeles CA 90095-1622
www.filmtv.ucla.edu
Tel: (310) 825-4321

9

USC School of Cinema-Television
Office of Admission
Attn: Production Program
University Park, CTV-G130
Los Angeles, CA 90089-2211
www.cntv.usc.edu
Tel: (213) 740-8358

10

The University of Texas at Austin
Department of Radio-TV-Film
1 University Station A0800
Austin, TX 78712-0108
www.utexas.edu/coc/rtf/
Tel: (512) 471-4071

ALTERNATIVES TO FILM SCHOOL

Not sold on film school? There are other avenues you might want to explore.

* *ART SCHOOL*

Especially for animators. "At art school, what was so great was that everybody was so supportive and not competitive with each other," raves Eileen O'Meara. "It was, 'How are you expressing yourself? How can we do it better? Let me help you. Borrow my paint brush.' I loved it."

* *FILM CLASSES AT A REGULAR UNIVERSITY*

Signing up for a one-off class allows you to take advantage of institutional learning without making the full film school commitment.

* *ASKING A FILM STUDENT TO PRODUCE YOUR SHORT*

You can benefit from some of his or her privileges (discounts) without having to pay for school yourself.

* *VOLUNTEERING TO WORK ON STUDENT PRODUCTIONS*

They're always glad for an extra hand, and you're making friends and contacts. And learning from their mistakes.

* *WATCHING A BUNCH OF DVDS*

Let's not forget the best film school of all — DVDs. Naturally, most of the flicks issued on DVD are much larger productions than you can ever hope to achieve with a short, but filmmaking is still filmmaking. You can learn a lot from the all-access pass that DVD bonus material provides.

TEN ESSENTIAL "FILM SCHOOLS IN A BOX"

If you're looking for film school in a box, these DVDs come highly recommended by short filmmakers and by the DVD review editors at *www.digitallyOBSESSED.com*.

1

EL MARIACHI

Filmmaker: Robert Rodriguez

Issued on DVD by Columbia/Tristar Home Video in 1998.

Robert Rodriguez is the patron saint of all no-budget filmmakers. On the *Director's Double Feature* version, which has both *El Mariachi* and *Desperado*, Rodriguez not only provides commentary, he includes bonus material such as his own short film, *Bedhead*, and his *10 Minute Film School*, in which he shows you how to make a film like *El Mariachi* for no money. You'll find the *10 Minute Film School* worth 10,000 hours of normal film school.

2

AMERICAN MOVIE

Filmmaker: Chris Smith

Issued on DVD by Columbia/Tristar Home Video in 2000.

Watch the documentary that chronicles the making of Mark Borchardt's short film, *Coven*. "The documentary was informed by the work that was being done," explains Borchardt. "Chris wasn't looking to make a documentary, but he saw the passion, the motivation, the energy that was being accumulated and fostered by this short film that just would not die and that had to be done under the most extreme circumstances. The material was like a gold chunk shining in everyone's faces, so the documentary cameras start to roll."

3

VISIONS OF LIGHT: THE ART OF CINEMATOGRAPHY

Filmmakers: Stuart Samuels, Todd McCarthy, and Arnold Glassman

Issued on DVD by Image Entertainment in 2000.

Watching this documentary about cinematography will make you a better director. Listen to what the masters have to say, watch what they achieved, and apply those lessons to your own filmmaking.

4

HEARTS OF DARKNESS: A FILMMAKER'S APOCALYPSE

Filmmakers: Fax Bahr, George Hickenlooper, and Eleanor Coppola
This 1991 documentary is out of print, but used DVD copies still can be acquired on Amazon or eBay.

And you thought making a short film was going to be tough! Watch this documentary on the making of *Apocalypse Now* and realize that you've got it easy. It will also cure you of any inclination to be too ambitious.

5

LOST IN LA MANCHA

Filmmakers: Keith Fulton and Louis Pepe
Issued on DVD by New Video Group in 2003.

Another "feature film production gone terribly wrong" favorite. Be grateful your problems are so much smaller in scale than Terry Gilliam's.

6

FIGHT CLUB

Filmmaker: David Fincher
Issued on DVD in a two-disc package by Twentieth Century Fox Home Entertainment in 2000.

The special edition includes an entire second disc including seventeen behind-the-scenes vignettes. After watching and listening to all the supplementary material, you'll be inspired to be as creative as director David Fincher.

7

BRAM STOKER'S DRACULA

Filmmaker: Francis Ford Coppola
Issued on DVD by Columbia/Tristar Home Video in 2000.

Short filmmaker Robbie Consing is a huge fan of this DVD. "The behind-the-scenes show Coppola doing the rehearsals, shooting the rehearsals, and then plugging sound effects in the animatic [moving storyboards]," Consing says. "Now, that may look huge and elaborate and intimidating, but picture your friends instead of Gary Oldman and Winona Ryder, and picture your own drawings alongside the music from *Dracula*, and you realize you can do this, too."

8
AMERICAN BEAUTY (THE AWARDS EDITION)
Filmmaker: Sam Mendes
Issued on DVD by Universal Studios in 2003

Bob Mandel and the digitallyOBSESSED.com editors rave, "Aside from being Sam Mendes' first feature, the supplements include the director in conversation with the screenwriter and the director of photography. Very useful and hands-on stuff."

9
SECRETARY
Filmmaker: Steven Shainberg
Issued on DVD by Lions Gate Home Entertainment in 2003.

Another recommendation from *www.digitallyOBSESSED.com*: "Lots of practical stuff on the commentary track — bits about the production design and the costume people, for instance. Also, a film made on a very tight budget."

10
THE LORD OF THE RINGS - THE FELLOWSHIP OF THE RING (PLATINUM SERIES SPECIAL EXTENDED EDITION)
Filmmaker: Peter Jackson.
Issued on DVD on four discs by New Line Home Video in 2002.

Everyone recommends this box set as the ultimate film school in a box. Spread out over four discs, the special features take you throughout the filmmaking process. Watch this and picture yourself one day helming such a grand production. It can happen.

Also:

The *www.digitallyOBSESSED.com* editors lobby one last suggestion: "Watch any of the Robert Altman movies with a commentary track — maybe *M*A*S*H* or *Gosford Park* — because every director, first-time or otherwise, wants to be as loved by his or her actors as Altman is."

READY TO DIRECT?

Even if you went to film school, inside every director is that gnawing doubt that says, "Who am I to be claiming to be the next Spielberg? I'll never be as talented as David Fincher. How can I call myself a director? I don't even own a baseball cap!" Don't panic. Remember, you don't need a diploma or a license to be a director. You're the studio. You've decided hiring you to be the director is a good decision. If you believe in you, others will follow suit. Don't worry, you'll be fine.

TEN THINGS EVERY DIRECTOR SHOULD KNOW

There is no real rule book for directing, but if you want to act like a real director, here are some helpful tips.

1
ALWAYS REMEMBER YOU'RE NOT CURING CANCER.
Obvious, but easy to forget.

2
BE AN EGOIST.
"The thing I've learned about directors is you have to have a massive ego," reports Robbie Consing, who in addition to being a short filmmaker has worked as a storyboard artist for major directors such as Steven Spielberg, David Fincher, Michael Bay, and John Woo. "You don't have to display it, but you have to have it. Because you have to make these crew people and actors suffer endlessly to achieve your vision. If you're doing your own short with your own money, the one thing you want to be able to do at this point in your life is tell your story your way. Even if you don't know how to do it. Even if you're fudging your way through it. The point is this is the last time that you can call your own shots because you're the director and the producer. Once people start paying your tab, that's it. It becomes a question of how much are you wanting to fight for your own art. Making shorts is not the time to start chickening out. Because that doesn't say much about the rest of your life."

3
BUT DON'T BE A JERK.

Filmmaker Mat Fuller reminds us what's important. "I'm all about the thanks — 'Thanks, man!'," yells Fuller. "I can't remember ever in my life going, 'Thank God I was a jerk to that guy or I wouldn't have gotten what I wanted!' Until that happens, I'm not going to use that method. Just because you get to play director for a few days, don't be a jerk."

4
DON'T TRY TO DO EVERYTHING YOURSELF.

Why bite off more than you can comfortably chew? "It's essential that you have a great producer, and I would recommend not doing that yourself," advises filmmaker Amy Talkington. "It can be done, but it doubles the stress and it takes away your focus from directing. I worked as an assistant director on a short a friend of mine was directing and producing. As she was also the line producer, in between directing the actors she had to dole out petty cash. No. Not a good idea."

5
PICK YOUR PEOPLE WISELY.

Moviemaking is not a solitary proposition. Cast everyone — actors and crew — with care. "I was co-producing an ultra-low budget film several years ago, and we saved money by getting much of our crew for free," shares producer Melissa Brantley. "One of those free crewmembers was our script supervisor, who had never done a film before. When we interviewed her, we were not 100% comfortable with her abilities, but because we were excited about saving money and pushed for time we hired her anyway. After a very long fifth day of filming, when the crew was wrapped and we all were exhausted and had gone home, the producer and I get a dreaded call. On her way home, the script supervisor had put her notebook containing all of the script notes from the days before on top of her car and didn't realize it until she was going down the freeway, looked in her rearview mirror, and noticed papers flowing in the traffic behind her. I learned the hard way to always follow your gut, don't scrimp on the most important elements, and interview, interview, interview until you find qualified people. Qualified people do work for free if they know you are loyal and will take them with you when you succeed. Also, I learned not to push the crew so hard that they are completely exhausted and can't do great work."

5
INVOLVE YOUR CREW.
"Nobody's getting paid. They're just wanting to make a movie," Mat Fuller points out. "If you get everyone stoked, it's not like the director is over here and the grips are over there. On my shoot, the grip department had a full storyboard and shot breakdown showing what to do three weeks before we rolled film. A day we didn't get a shot, there were grip guys who were bummed."

7
BE PREPARED. BE ORGANIZED.
Yes, being a director is a lot like being a boy scout. As you've learned from watching *Hearts of Darkness* and *Lost in La Mancha*, so many things can go wrong in production. The only preventive thing you can do is be as ready as you can be. Don't let the problem on the set be you.

8
ENJOY THE PROCESS.
Life After Death director Jordan Horowitz is the first to admit that he gets "so freakin' stressed out making films that I almost find myself paralyzed on set, unable to accomplish what needs to be done. I think if you don't love the actual process of making the film, then there really is no point to doing it. It's very important how the finished product turns out, but remember, it's not where you are when you die, but how you enjoyed the process of living."

9
TAKE CARE OF YOURSELF PHYSICALLY.
Directing means being on your feet all day, usually outside, in changing temperature. Even if you're only doing a one-day shoot, you'll be much sharper if you don't exhaust yourself. I don't want to sound like your mother, but don't forget to eat. Drink plenty of water. Faithfully apply your sunscreen and lip balm. Wear comfortable shoes and layers. Whenever you can, sit down. You want to live to direct again, don't you?

10
WEAR A BASEBALL CAP.

Not only because a hat will protect you from the sun. Not only because you'll be so focused on directing you can't spend extra time worrying about your hair. Wear a baseball cap because you've watched enough of the behind-the-scene pieces on DVD to know wearing such a hat really does make you look like a director!

SHORT RECAP

- Film school is always an option.

- You can learn a lot from watching the bonus features and listening to director commentary on DVDs.

- Directors must have egos, but shouldn't be jerks.

- Surround yourself with capable people.

- Take care of yourself so you can be the best filmmaker you can be.

CHAPTER 5

WHAT KIND OF FILM SHOULD YOU MAKE?

Make the kind of film that you want to make, can make, and should make.

When Dave Silver came up with the idea for his film *Gasline*, he didn't think, "Ah, this will win me the 2002 Jury Award at the Sundance Film Festival!" It just so happened that it did. But Silver's real motivation was his love of storytelling. He wanted to capture on film something he had remembered from growing up during the 1970s. The result was a sixteen-minute tale about a gas station during a fuel shortage.

"Stay true to the film you want to make," advises Trevor Groth, senior programmer at the Sundance Film Festival. "There aren't any boundaries or set rules that you have to follow. That's the beauty of a short. It's whatever you want to make it. Just stay true to your passion and tell the story you want to tell."

John Halecky, former Director of Development at IFILM.com, agrees. "At IFILM, we would always tell filmmakers don't alter your ideas because you think your film might not look as good on the web, or you don't think a distributor will buy it, or it may not play well at festivals. If you do that, then you're not making the film you want to make. Just tell a good story. And make it something that people want to watch."

AMAZE US

In most cases, short filmmakers have the kind of absolute creative freedom that feature directors dream of. Because you are your own studio, you control your own budget, get final cut, and have total say on marketing.

Because the format itself has no rules regarding length, structure, or content, anything goes. "You'll see stuff you couldn't imagine," marvels Sundance's Groth.

Take the Jesus film, for example. While poor Martin Scorsese was practically crucified for making the controversial feature *The Last Temptation of Christ*, short filmmakers fearlessly produce much more outrageous Christ stories all the time. Who can forget *Spirit of Christmas*, in which Jesus wrestles Santa in front of an audience of profanity-spewing South Park boys? Perhaps because Jesus is such an established figure that filmmakers don't have to waste time creating his character, Christ shows up in a wide variety of short films. Just when I thought Jesus Christ has been used in every possible way, a student in my short film class shocked me by showing his film in which Hitler is revealed to be Christ. As I told the director at the time, "I've seen a lot of shorts with Jesus, and I've seen a lot with Hitler, but this is the first I've seen them together." If you want to make a short about Jesus (or Hitler), go ahead. Just be original and unique.

AND THEN THERE WAS STAR WARS

John Halecky, who has worked at several dot-com short film companies, laughingly offers up a mock formula for guaranteed success — at least with male viewers on the Internet. "If you're making a short film that you really want to get a lot of eyes to, it better be about sex or *Star Wars*. If you make one that has sex <u>and</u> *Star Wars*, you've got a hit on your hands!"

It's obvious why sex is popular, but why *Star Wars*? Probably because it's a film that continues to be a touchstone for generations of filmmakers. And like Jesus, everyone knows the characters, what they look like and represent.

So let's say you want to make a *Star Wars* homage film. If you're Kevin Rubio with access to extensive postproduction favors and a costumer who can pull together very realistic storm trooper uniforms on a penny, then you can achieve something like *Troops*, a "what if you do *Cops* with storm troopers?" noodle of an idea that became an eleven-minute cult classic. If you're Joe Nussbaum with a production company willing to finance a fairly big budget shoot and a friend who looks a lot like young George Lucas, you can pull off a slick *Shakespeare in Love* parody called *George Lucas in*

Love. Or if you're Ernie Fosselius, a visionary genius who pioneered the *Star Wars* parody business with *Hardware Wars*, you could create perhaps one of the most enduring, beloved and financially successful low-rent shorts of all time.

There are a million ways to do a riff on *Star Wars*. If you want to do one, first come up with an original twist, then evaluate whether you can bring your concept off. Do you have the skills, resources, and finances to do it right? If not, you can still give it your best shot, but be aware that many superior filmmakers have already beat you to the punch — do you really want to compete against *George Lucas in Love, Troops,* or *Hardware Wars* with inferior material?

If the piece you really want to do is something beyond your capabilities at this point in time, put it aside until you are ready. In the meantime, think of another piece that you can do and do well. Then attempt your grand masterpiece as your next project. If you still want to.

THINK AHEAD

The important thing to remember is the film you make does brand you. Shorts are a way of establishing your persona as a filmmaker. Filmmaker David Birdsell made a short featuring a pug; Hollywood studio executives offered him dog projects. If your ultimate goal is to be directing *My Friend Flicka* remakes for the Disney Channel, doing a *Star Wars* parody is probably not the best use of your resources.

THINK ORGANICALLY

So before you begin your filmmaking career, take an assessment of who you are and where you want to go. Once you know that (and that's big), look at what you actually can do.

First, list five feature films you wished you had made. What do they have in common? This should help define your personal style. If you wanted to make a film similar to those films, what would you need? If you like dramatic character pieces, you'll need a strong story, good dialogue, and talented actors. If you like war movies, your story might be inspired by a visit to the local army surplus store where you can score free props and wardrobe. You get the idea.

Let's say you have the perfect idea for a short — it's something unique and special, reflects your taste, and shows potential employers what you can you do. But realistically, you'll have to shoot for five days, feeding at least twenty people. Even if there were no other cost but $10 a meal for twenty people for five days, you need $1,000 to get through production. If you don't have a grand, you can either wait until you can raise that money, or you can come up with another idea that you can do well within your means.

Don't get sold on one idea that you must, must, must make. There are millions of ideas out there. It's like shopping. You have to take a bunch of stuff into the dressing room, try them all on, and only buy what looks best on you. Perhaps you need to put something back on the rack and shop around just to make sure, then come back later to purchase it.

Take filmmaker Noah Edelson, for example. He's a funny guy who has a hundred funny ideas for a short film. He's got one called *He Had a Hat*. It starts with an old lady walking down the beach with her baseball cap-wearing grandson (please note that Noah is the one who complains that all shorts begin with someone walking somewhere — and here his film starts with someone walking!). All of a sudden a huge wave crashes to shore and drags the little boy out to sea. The old woman drops to her knees and prays. Her dialogue is something like "Dear God, I'll be eternally grateful if you bring my grandson back alive." Another huge wave hits, this time returning the little boy, who is sopping wet but miraculously alive. The old lady's responds (to God), "He had a hat!"

Noah lives in Los Angeles, so the beach isn't a problem, nor are the actors. The problem? The huge wave. Unlike *Troops* director Kevin Rubio or the *405* guys, Noah doesn't know special effects people who could do this for him for free. He could have made some cold calls to companies that specialize in CGI, getting through the nos until he found a yes, but he decided to put this idea aside and do something that didn't require CGI. By the way, Noah still might do *He Had a Hat* one day, so don't steal the idea!

TEN CATEGORIES OF SHORT FILMS

If you're shopping around for a short film to make, you might be inspired by these tried and true formulas.

1

PARODY/HOMAGE

After *Star Wars*, the feature film that inspired the most parodies in recent years is *The Blair Witch Project*. For a while *Blair Witch* variations were quite the ticket, partially because the low budget film is easy to ape, but mostly because it did indeed inspire many wannabe filmmakers to actually pick up a video camera and give it a shot.

You can take almost any feature film and find a way to lampoon it. One notorious example was *Saving Ryan's Privates*. As you can probably surmise, it had a lot of penis jokes. A parody can do very well in Hollywood and very often land the filmmaker an agent ("funny is money," as they say). It's also an easy way to come up with an idea because you don't have to start from scratch.

If you sit down and think for five minutes, you can probably come up with a parody that you can easily knock off for no money with a borrowed DV camera. Brainstorming parodies in my 2003 short film class, filmmaker Jakob White came up with *My Big Fat Hillbilly Wedding* (don't steal the idea if he hasn't made it yet).

Why not shoot a quick parody, just for kicks? Submit it to *ifilm.com* or *atomfilms.com*, see what happens. Meanwhile, you'll be even more confident about tackling your "real film" having logged some experience behind the camera.

One caveat: parodies don't do well on the festival circuit. "A parody, however loving and funny it can be, is often something that capitalizes on the moment and that's all it has to offer," explains Palms Springs International Festival of Short Films programmer Thomas Harris. "In other words, there are very few *George Lucas in Loves*. That film is an all-out creative original approach to telling the backstory of how *Star Wars* came to exist. And it's a very good film, very good filmmaking. But most people are taking the conceits of *Memento* or whatever, and they're just riffing on them. I always feel a little empty inside when I watch a parody. And I wonder where the creativity went."

2

ADAPTED WORKS

Many short filmmakers want to adapt something that already exists, such as a classic short story. Parodies you can do without getting permission (although you do have to be careful about copyrighted or trademarked elements), but fashioning a legitimate adaptation of previously published material requires permission.

Let's say you want to adapt a Stephen King story. To go about it properly, you need to contact King's representative. To do this, you look to see which company originally published the book or short story, then call that publishing house (most big publishing houses are in New York). Ask to speak to the subsidiary rights department. Because that department is deluged with phone calls, you'll most likely get a recording that will tell you to fax your request and someone will get back to you.

Fax a request to the subsidiary rights department saying you are interested in the film and television rights to the particular Stephen King story. Make sure you include all of your contact information so they can get back to you either by fax, phone, or e-mail.

You'll mostly likely be given the name of an agent who represents the author for film and television sales. Call that agent and explain that you would like to adapt the story as a short film. Naturally, agents are in the business of generating revenue for their authors and taking a percentage of that revenue as their payment. So you might imagine an agent, who has many clients and many money deals in various stages of negotiation, might not be thrilled to hear from you, a nobody filmmaker wanting to get the rights to adapt his client's story for free.

Some agents will be extremely unhelpful. You'll have to win them over with your passion for the material. One way is to make it impossible to say no to you. If you can draw amazing storyboards, you might storyboard out your version of the film and mail it to the agent, who will hopefully feel obliged to send it on to King rather than trashing it. You hope, then, that King will be equally impressed.

What exactly are you asking for when you contact the writer's representative? You can ask for the ultimate — exclusive rights to adapt the original work in all formats, in perpetuity, throughout the universe — just like you would for a feature film. In reality, very few people will grant you such permission. Why should they?

Here are the two words you need to know because you will use them time and time again as you approach rights holders: "gratis" — which is a fancy way of saying "free" — and "nonexclusive." Nonexclusive means Stephen King can grant the film rights to the story to you, to the next guy who asks, and anyone and everyone who comes along down the line. Therefore, King's not losing any money by giving it to you for free because he still maintains the rights to sell it to another filmmaker who might come along one day with money. Of course, the only reason anyone will do this is if you promise you're not commercially exploiting the original work for financial gain. Because if there's money involved, people want to get paid. Instead, you're asking only for permission to make a piece of art that is a learning experience and which will only be shown in festival settings. Many short filmmakers have been able to score nonexclusive festival rights for gratis from pretty big authors.

Before you start tracking down King's agent, think about whether you really should do an adaptation. Although the obvious advantage is that there's a built-in interest factor in a King adaptation (festivals will want to book it because they know audiences will be interested), you won't necessarily benefit. If people like the film, they'll ascribe all the good things to King. Additionally, if you do a great job with your adaptation, you'll get offers from television stations and DVD companies to license the film, but you'll be hamstrung by your agreement with King not to commercially exploit the film. Although you say you don't care about commercial exhibition now, you will once you're in massive credit card debt and people are dangling a few thousand in front of you.

Naturally, works that are in the public domain don't require permission. But you still have the problem that people will say, "Sure she did a good adaptation of *Occurrence at Owl Creek Bridge*, but can she come up with an original idea of her own?" Save adaptations for later. Find something you want to adapt into a feature, then when you get meetings with Hollywood executives based on your outstanding original short film and they ask you if you have something you want to do next, bring up the adaptation. Make the studio execs do the leg work of securing the rights for you. Have them pay you to do the adaptation. That's a much better plan of action.

3
MOCUMENTARY

Mocumentaries work particularly well in the short format. They're also a good aesthetic fit if you want to shoot on DV and have it look professional. Director Brian McDonald had great success with *White Face*, which he shot for a grand and has earned him a hundred times its budget back. "It's weird because it didn't help me the way I thought it would, as a sample of my writing and directing," McDonald admits. "Because the way the film is, I really worked hard to get very natural performances and to adhere to the documentary form. So people think the performances are improv — even though it's fully scripted, and the script won an award, and the movie is almost exactly like the script. People think, 'Well, the actors made it up, and Brian caught it on film.' So the film actually does better than I do! For example, I had a major star's production company call me after they saw the movie. They said, 'You know we just can't tell if you can direct from this film.' The problem is it's a mocumentary. Next time, I have to make a film that looks like a film."

4
WEEKEND PRODUCTION

There is a magic formula that many short filmmakers swear by — including me. I firmly believe making a weekend short is the best way to get the most bang for your buck. If you rent equipment on Friday, you only pay one rental day and you can keep everything until Monday morning. You can easily recruit crew and actors for the weekend because you're not impinging on their work week. Ditto locations.

The most economical weekend shoot is one day, one location. The second is two days, one location. Lastly, one or two days, many locations. Knowing these boundaries, can you come up with a story you can do well? If you like these constraints, you might go the extra yard and apply for the various forty-eight hour film contests that a lot of festivals are sponsoring. Many people find having to shoot and edit an entire film in two days can be creatively freeing. If you're interested, there's a traveling contest called The 48 Hour Film Project. Visit the *www.48hourfilm.com* web site for more information.

5
LOCATION-INSPIRED STORY

Is there an intriguing location that you can get free access to? Can you create a story around it? David Birdsell found this odd street in down-town Los Angeles when he was scouting for his first short, *Blue City*. He was fasci-

nated by the two palm trees in the middle of that industrial setting. When it came time to make a second film, the Fox Movie Channel short *Phil Touches Flo*, he set his story on that street.

6
PERSONALITY-INSPIRED SHOWCASE

Do you know someone who deserves to be in pictures? Write something for him to star in. Or perhaps you're an actor creating a showcase for yourself. If that's the case, make sure you do yourself justice. Before he was a big movie star, Vin Diesel wrote, directed, and acted in a short he called *Multifacial*. The flick starts off with Vin telling a story about proposing to his girlfriend in a restaurant. The reveal is that he's actually auditioning for a part in a movie. The short becomes a series of auditions, none of which he gets because he's either too black, too white, too Italian, etc. *Multifacial* is not only a great showcase for Vin's range as an actor, it has something to say about identity and race. It was on the basis of that short that Spielberg cast Diesel in *Saving Private Ryan*.

7
A JOKE

As filmmaker Noah Edelson well knows, jokes with strong punch lines ("He had a hat!") work well as short films. Urban myths also translate extremely well. Francine McDougall's *Pig!* is prime example. *Pig!* begins with a snooty woman driving her Mercedes up a winding rural road. Coming down the road in the other direction is a motorscooter driven by a gross guy picking his nose. She yells out to the nosepicker, "Pig!" Cut to the sound of a crash. The motorscooter is flipped on its side as a big snorting pig wanders around in the middle of the road. That film did very well on the festival circuit. Filmmaker Roy Unger, who made a dark moody flick called *Requiem*, came to realize that "if you want to make short, think comedy because that's what get programmed a lot. Comedies kill in film festivals. A good funny comedy, that is. There's nothing worse than bad comedy. With bad drama, viewers can think they just don't get it. But with comedy, people either laugh or they don't. If they don't laugh, that's an ugly silence! If you're going to do a comedy, make it funny."

8

SKILL-INSPIRED DEMO PIECE

Do you have a skill that you want to show off to get future work? Display your wares. Come up with a short that will also function as a demo. Perfect example: the guys who made *405* used computer programs such as LightWave 3D by Newtek, Digital Fusion by Eyeon Software, Adobe Photoshop, Adobe Premiere and Illusion to make a heavily computer-generated short that rivals Michael Bay blockbusters. Needless to say, they got a lot of work off of that flick!

9

INTERNET/NEW DEVICES SENSATION

Not all shorts have to be geared toward festivals. Many are Internet sensations (again, think *405*). "Obviously, one of the most important things to remember if you want your film on the Internet, shorter is better," counsels AtomFilms.com's Megan O'Neill. "Comedies work very well. Also flash animation, and animation in general. Having said that, we've had some very serious documentaries about 9/11 that have done tremendous traffic. One of the most popular films at Atom is *Voice of a Prophet*, about a man who ended up dying in 9/11. He was a security person at Morgan Stanley. Tremendous, tremendous reviews and traffic. So sometimes films surprise you. Titles definitively matter online. We have a short by Amy Talkington called *Our Very First Sex Tape*, which has done tremendously well. When people see 'sex' in the title, they go right to that! *405* is an excellent example of an online film, of a film that fits the medium. It's very well lit, very well shot — you can actually see everything. Too many films are so dark you actually can't see anything when you put them online."

Filmmaker Tara Veneruso has made shorts for both the Internet and new devices. "Something that is going to be on a new device like a palm pilot or cell phone needs to be under two minutes long," Veneruso explains. "It has to be something that someone can fast forward through, and it will have the same effect. Sound is extremely compressed, so minimal dialogue is good. Certain things work really well: parodies, comedies, but also experimental. In general, things you might imagine seeing on an old-fashioned nickelodeon work well on new devices."

10
A SHORT THAT WANTS TO BE A FEATURE

Bottle Rocket began life as a short film. So did *Raising Victor Vargas* (the short was called *Five Feet High and Rising*). *Fatal Attraction. House Party. Slingblade.* You can make a short that is either part of a larger project, or a short that can obviously be developed into a feature project.

Or you can make a short that is as ambitious in scope as a feature but is constrained by the short format. There are plusses and minuses to doing that. Columbia grad Amy Talkington recalls, "My first student film was eighteen minutes long and it was sort of unresolved. It was an example of a feature story that was trying to be a short film. A lot of feature producers were interested in talking to me about features because, while it wasn't the most successful short, it did display the ability to create a more complicated story and a more complicated character. It wasn't that successful of a short film, so it didn't make that leap for me, but it did get me some interest."

SHORT RECAP

- Stay true to your passion and tell the story you want to tell.

- Take advantage of the form's creative freedom to make something that is original and unique to you.

- It's better to mount a realistically scaled production that plays to your strengths rather than attempt a too-ambitious project that you can't do well.

- Don't make a film in a specific genre/style if that's not the direction you see yourself heading in the future.

- Your film will be judged against those that have come before it. Aim to make the best film you possibly can.

CHAPTER 6

TO DV OR NOT TO DV

***DV** is your most accessible format, but shooting on film shouldn't be ruled out.*

Ask even the most staunch supporters of shooting on film, and they'll admit that DV is great for short filmmakers. It's easy, accessible, and perfect for experimentation. Even major DPs are willing to shoot digital. Before you jump on the bandwagon, let's look at the pros and cons of every format. Because while features remain tethered to 35mm, short filmmakers can indulge in a wide range of formats.

70MM

Let's start big: IMAX. Mark Osborne shot his animated film *More* on 65mm/15 perf film stock for 70mm/15 perf projection, and his short ran for six months with the blockbuster *Everest* in IMAX theaters in New York and London. Talk about filmmaker nirvana! "Just to clarify," Osborne edifies, "IMAX is a brand name, Giant Screen is the generic term. 15 perf refers to the size of the 70mm film used (it's running horizontal so the image is 15 perfs across, unlike the regular 70mm film you usually hear about which runs vertically at 5 perfs wide). 65mm is the shooting stock, and 70mm is the release stock." If your dream is theatrical exhibition before paying audiences, Giant Screen format might be your ideal way to go.

PROS OF SHOOTING GIANT SCREEN FORMAT
- Best resolution possible. A major plus for those filmmakers obsessed with great looking pictures.

- Strong marketing and exhibition hook. You're in your own category when you're making an IMAX short.

- Opportunity exists. Because only a rare few features use the large format, this is probably the only time in your career you'll get to deal with 70mm.

- Extended theatrical exhibition. If you can hook up with the IMAX folks.

- Possible Oscar nomination. The Academy acknowledges that IMAX short films are legitimately commercially exhibited films. In fact, *More* was nominated.

CONS OF SHOOTING GIANT SCREEN FORMAT

- Expensive. Filmstock, lab services, and slower pace of production cause large format productions to be costlier. Osborne estimates his budget would have been half a million if he hadn't gotten many goods and services donated.

- Unwieldy cameras. However, there are models that can go on Steadicams.

- Inaccessible equipment. Unlike the more commonplace cameras gathering dust at your local rental house, the cameras designed to handle IMAX-style shooting are being used by productions in remote areas like Mount Everest or China. Good luck begging one for the weekend!

- Postproduction nightmares. There are a limited number of specialized labs that work in 70mm, and digital effects require higher final resolutions (more time and more money).

- Limited Giant Screen exhibition opportunities. Because most film festivals won't have access to an IMAX theater, your film won't be shown in its ideal format. Additionally, most people will ultimately see your short on TV, DVD, or the Internet, never knowing it was shot in such a superior format.

35MM

This is the format you will probably spend the rest of your filmmaking career working in, so why not get your feet wet now? You'll love it, your DP will love it, your cast will love it, film festivals will love it, sales agents will love it. "There's something about 35mm that demands attention," proclaims filmmaker George Langworthy. What's the downside? It's expensive to shoot film, and 35mm is more expensive than 16mm.

"I am pro 35," says filmmaker Mat Fuller, who shot his flick *Deveria* on that format. "With 35mm, you're going to do a short that really shows what you can do. But it cost so much, and Panavision cameras cost as well. If you're not going to screen on film, you don't need the extra resolution that 35 has, and 16mm will totally tide you over to get to a video master. But then with 16, you've got the depth of field issue. The first thing that marks something as a student film — or a cheap film — is that everything is in focus all the time. With 35mm, you can get your depth of field to drop off quick."

PROS OF SHOOTING 35MM

- Professional format. There's a whole different vibe on the set when it's a 35mm shoot — it says this is a "real movie."

- Format you'll probably use for future feature work. Learn how to make 35mm films from the start.

- Looks great. You and your Director of Photography will be happy.

- Easily projected. Festivals love to screen 35mm since 16mm projectors are becoming relics.

- Freebies moderately easy to score. Because so many productions use 35mm, there are more place you can hit up to borrow equipment and get deals.

CONS OF SHOOTING 35MM

- Cameras not readily available. Many DPs own their own 16mm or DV cameras, but have to rent 35mm. Additionally, the 35mm cameras aren't just sitting on the shelves like the less popular 16mms.

- Unwieldy. You can't just climb up a pole, strap on roller-skates to do dolly shots, or board a bus without a permit like you can with the smaller format cameras.

- Consumes a lot of film stock. You'll need to secure more feet of film than you would if you were shooting with 16mm. 35mm film has sixteen frames per foot and runs ninety feet per minute, while 16mm has forty frames per foot and runs thirty-six feet per minute. You do the math.

- Sizeable crew needed. There's no one-man-band-style shooting with 35mm.

- Requires auxiliary equipment. We're talking lenses, filters, lighting packages, dolly, camera mounts, etc.

16MM

While only the most independent feature films still shoot 16mm or Super-16, short filmmakers (especially those in film school) still enjoy the smaller format.

Filmmaker Jordan Horowitz explains his fondness for 16mm. "I'm a film guy, and just don't think I'm capable of making a good film that's shot on video, even if it's the 24p Hi-Def cameras," says Horowitz. "Super-16 is a great format, especially since you can still get all of the same stocks as 35mm. What I've learned is that it's all about the transfer. I've seen 16mm films mastered onto DigiBeta or BetaSP that look as good as anything else, but I've also tried saving money and going to DVCAM, and this really does damage the quality of the image."

Another 16mm proponent is *Breezeway* director George Langworthy. "If I were to shoot on film, I would never shoot on 35. I would shoot on 16. Probably not Super-16. But maybe. It depends on what I was doing. A cool black-and-white 16mm short could really kick ass. Feature films can't be in black and white (unless you're doing *Schindler's List* and you're Spielberg) — it's one of the things shorts can do. It would look great, and you would not go totally broke. You could probably fit it onto one credit card. In fact, 16 is pretty cheap these days because all the equipment is just sitting around. You can get a camera for nothing. To shoot about ten minutes of 16 will cost you about $400. When you transfer to video, the aspect ratio fits perfectly. And you can still get that beautiful latitude. My friend Dan Loflin, who did a short called *Delusions of Modern Primitivism*, shot on 16mm. I think it's a brilliant example. Didn't bump up to 35mm. That's the key. That costs a jillion bucks. He kept it on 16mm. And boy, with that film in particular, there's no way in hell he could have shot on video — he's shooting directly into the sun half the time when the lead character is riding around. What I found with film is this: If you shoot a short on film, 90% of the people are going to see it on video ultimately. So with 16mm, you have the advantages of film, but it's cheaper than 35."

If you stay 16mm as a film print, be aware that the sound in the theaters will be sub par and you'll be ghettoized with the 16mm features and shorts programs. "I hear filmmakers all the time saying, 'We should have done it on 35!'," reports film sales agent Carol Crowe of Apollo Cinema. "Because not only does it look better in the theater, it's better sound with 35mm. Overall, it's really hard to compete when you shoot on 16. So I say don't bother doing 16. Certainly most theaters have done away with those projectors, and multiplexes can't platter a 16."

PROS OF SHOOTING 16MM

- Smaller, more portable camera than 35mm.

- Can usually get camera for free.

- Requires less crew.

- Film stock cheap. Processing cheap.

- Aspect ratio fits TV.

CONS OF SHOOTING 16MM

- Lesser format than 35mm. If you can get 35mm for free, why step down the food chain to use 16? You won't be using 16mm for the rest of your career, so why start with it?

- Smaller negative. 16mm is less than half the size of 35mm, so you're giving up a lot of resolution.

- Blowing up to 35mm is expensive.

- Poor sound capacity on 16mm prints.

• Limited projection opportunities. Film print screenings are limited to places that still have 16mm projectors.

8MM

Let's not forget the old and trusty friend of generations of short filmmakers: 8mm. Why shoot 8mm when video is so prevalent? Filmmaker George Langworthy explains that "the crucial difference between film and video is the latitude — the difference between the lightest and darkest image that the film or video can record. On video, it's much smaller. Your range of light is much more limited. For example, say you have someone standing in a dark room by a window, and it's really sunny outside. If you're shooting that on video, you can either have the outside image be visible and the person inside would be in complete black silhouette, or you could have the person be visible and the window totally blown out white. Whereas if you shoot that same image with Super-8, you can get everything: the person's face, the subtleties of what's going on inside the room, and the brightly lit exterior. Plus, the image quality has a unique look. They have these computer programs which will supposedly make things shot on video look like Super-8, but it really doesn't. Because you don't have the same kind of latitude. The resolution is different. It doesn't have the right rhythm. It just doesn't look the same."

Why else does Langworthy recommend 8mm? "Cameras are readily available, obviously. It's very easy to find Super-8 cameras, so you might as well get a good one. It's just like with video cameras today. There are the lower grade, consumer level ones, and there are the very advanced ones. Generally, with the more advanced ones you have more manual settings — control over your focus, your exposure, your zoom, etc. If you have a really good camera, you can rewind and do double exposures. The film itself is very cheap, something like $15 dollars a roll. You can get the film directly from Kodak, or most major cities have camera stores that will carry stock. For processing, you can just mail it. You can have it converted to a digital format so you can do digital editing. Personally, I just bought a good projector so I can project my footage on to a blank wall and shoot it with my DV camera as a way to transfer it myself. For both cameras and projectors, I would highly recommend eBay. And of course the web has several excellent Super-8 resource sites, such as *www.super8guy.com/Super8/DirectoryII.html* and *www.geocities.com/meta8mm.*"

But wait, there are even more great things about Super-8. "Super-8 film-making clubs have these one-reel competitions," Langworthy explains. "The filmmakers have to do what is called in-camera editing. It's a very nice way to make a film. You do the edit as you shoot, so you have to think every-thing out and really plan out your film. When you're done shooting a reel, you get it developed, and you're done! The film is edited, cut, and ready to look at. Of course, there's no sound. That's why Super-8 is so closely tied in with music. One of the real joys is discovering when you put your reel up against music, any music, magic happens. You'll find that what you've shot synchronizes with music in amazing ways. And it's really fun. That's absolutely the key word. Your effort involved is very little, and it's all about fun. Super-8 is affordable, accessible, cheap, fun, beautiful, works lovely in the short format. Super-8 filmmakers are doing it for the joy of filmmaking."

PROS OF SHOOTING 8MM

- Own and operate your own camera.

- Film is ridiculously cheap.

- Beautiful aesthetic.

- Very inexpensive to get a film print or to transfer footage to DV.

- Super-8 film clubs. A fun way to meet other filmmakers and have your work shown.

CONS OF SHOOTING 8MM

- Not professional format.

- Not "commercial" format. More of an art format.

- Very small negative size.

- No sound.

- Projection restricted. Film festivals — other than Super-8 fests — can't project 8mm.

PIXELVISION

What's the video equivalent of Super-8 (i.e., a camera of the past, which has become a beloved tool for short filmmakers)? Yes, it's pixelvision.

The actual camera is called the PXL-2000, which sounds very impressive, but in reality it's a kid's camera that records video on standard audio cassettes to create pixelvision. The resulting footage is black and white and runs at fifteen frames per second (as opposed to NTSC video's thirty fps). The name most associated with pixelvision is lesbian filmmaker Sadie Benning, who as a young girl in the late 1980s was given the camera by her father, an experimental filmmaker. The best commercially available example is Michael Almereyda's vampire feature, *Nadja* (1995), which has segments shot in pixelvision. Almereyda also did a 1997 pixelvision short called *The Rocking Horse Winner*, based on the D.H. Lawrence story and starring Eric Stoltz.

Manufactured only in the late 1980s, the camera itself is no longer being sold but can easily be scored off eBay for a hundred dollars or so. Recording audio and video onto a normal audiocassette (ninety-minute tapes will hold twenty minutes of video), you can easily output your work directly from the camera with a standard RF cable. The original PXL-2000 packaging proclaims that the camera "lets kids create their wildest dreams," and indeed many short filmmakers have found the format delightful.

PROS OF SHOOTING PIXELVISION

- Own and operate your own camera.

- Tape stock ridiculously cheap.

- Very distinctive look.

- Has sound. (Not great sound, but sound.)

- Very easy to transfer to another video format.

CONS OF SHOOTING PIXELVISION

- Not professional format.

- Not "commercial" format.

- No range in look. Everything you shoot will be black-and-white pixels.

- Cameras are no longer being manufactured. You're out of luck if yours breaks.

- Can't be projected. The only way to get a film print of your pixelvision short is to do a tape-to-film transfer.

DIGITAL VIDEO FORMATS

24p, Hi-Def, DigiBeta, mini-DV — don't let the various formats fool you. You're still shooting video instead of film. If you can use the top of the line cameras, go for it. However, sometimes renting an HD camera will cost you as much as shooting film. In general, if you're committing yourself to shoot video (any format of video), you should shoot with whatever camera you can get your hands on.

A friend of mine showed me a short shot with a borrowed Canon XL1. My honest reaction was, "Looks cheap. Too bad you couldn't afford to shoot on film." My friend's mistake was making a traditional type of short that should have been shot on film if he wanted it to be a director's calling card. Digital video was chosen for economic rather than artistic reasons, and it showed. Just as an IMAX film has a different aesthetic than an 8mm flick, DV as a format has its own inherent properties that filmmakers must acknowledge. Film has a richness, reacts to light, and can handle depth of field in ways that video simply can't imitate. Because most DV films find their widest audience on the Internet rather than in the movie theatre, DV filmmakers would be wise to not worry about "film look" and spend their time exploring what DV can really do.

"For female directors especially, mini-DV is a really great tool," raves filmmaker Tara Veneruso. "Recently I took my little Canon GL1, which I love, and climbed up onto a streetlight post. I was grateful for the ability to have a camera that was so small and light weight. Whereas before, I might have to rely on the strength of a guy to lift the camera up and a guy to shoot it. Mini-DV is extremely portable. You can strap on rollerblades and it's like you have a built-in dolly. Put the camera on a boom stick, and you have your great aerial shot."

Keep in mind that a digital camera isn't a license to be lazy. You will be tempted to use the camera just like a regular video camera, i.e., hand-held, employing available light and sound. Go ahead, if that style of filmmaking suits your material. If you want a more polished look, you need to be more meticulous. In preproduction, do tests to familiarize yourself with your camera and what it can do. If your camera offers a "film look," make sure you're happy with it before you commit to using it. If you ever plan on bumping up to film via the fairly expensive tape-to-film process, don't use it. How does the in-camera microphone perform? If it isn't sufficient (most aren't), explore other options. During production, take the time to properly light and compose shots. You can make your footage look more "film-like" in editing by using programs such as Adobe After Effects, but lay the groundwork by shooting it properly in the first place. Don't overshoot just because "tape is cheap." You'll regret overindulging when you start editing and find yourself overwhelmed by too many options. Get the shot you need, then move on. But always review your footage before moving on. Is the sound okay? If you need to re-shoot, take care of it then and there.

"In this day and age, it's less of a question of to DV or not to DV," states *Sidewalkers* director Tara Veneruso. "Let's face it, we're all heading there whether we want to or not. So let's learn it now, and get used to the format. I think the questions should be: What camera do I use? If I were going to use film, is there really a significant reason to use film over DV? And maybe in a few years the questions will be entirely different — like is film still being made?"

PROS OF SHOOTING DV

- Own and operate your own camera. Mini-DV cameras, in particular, are much smaller, more portable, and less complicated than most film cameras.

- Tape stock cheaper than film.

- Very minimal crew needed. You really can do it all yourself if you shoot DV.

- Immediate gratification. You can look at your footage on set; no waiting to develop it to make sure everything's okay.

- Easy to load into desktop editing systems. You can firewire your footage directly into your computer from your camera.

CONS OF SHOOTING DV

- Considered by some to be less serious or less professional than film.

- Top of the line video cameras not as easy to get free as top of the line film cameras.

- DV can't capture the same quality or richness that film can. The hard, flat look can read as cheap.

- To strike a film print requires an expensive tape-to-film process.

- Evolving format. Digital video is only getting better, so your cutting edge DV short might look outdated almost immediately.

BAD ANIMALS: A DV PRODUCTION CASE STUDY

Let's get specific about how DV can be extremely liberating for the short filmmaker. When we were putting together the DVD short film collection, *Short 10: Chaos,* we commissioned filmmaker David Birdsell to make a short film with the theme of "chaos." Keeping in mind his contracted budget of $1,000, he came up with the following story. A man waits for the bus. Across the street, a person in a full-on chicken costume stares relentlessly at him. The chicken crosses the road, and continues to stare at the man, who is getting progressively freaked out. Luckily, the bus comes, and the man makes his escape. A few stops later, a person in a full-on mouse costume boards the bus and sits down, staring at the man. The mouse is so bold as to move to the seat right next to the man. Desperate to escape, the man jumps out at the next stop. Exiting onto the street, he's confronted by a person in a bear suit. The mouse also exits the bus, and the mouse and bear start shoving the man. The man runs away, pursued by the mouse and the bear. All of a sudden, his path is cut off by a huge 1970s-era convertible — driven by the chicken. The three animals wrestle the man to the ground, chloroform him, and dump his unconscious body into the convertible's trunk. The bad animals hop into the convertible and drive away. The end.

Because there was money involved, Birdsell didn't feel like he had to operate under the "Everything for Free!" mandate. He had cash to dispense, so he paid everyone who worked on the film, rented the car and costumes, and even splurged on a few toys. If you were producing this short for no money, you would have called every car rental place until you got the convertible for free, every costume shop until you got the costumes for free, etc. And of course everyone would have worked for free. Now, if you were shooting it with a 35mm camera, you'd have to call the bus company, see if you could rent the bus for the day, pay the driver, get friends to be extras, lug the 35mm camera up into the bus, etc. But David Birdsell knew he was going to borrow a mini-DV camera and be his own crew. David was willing to risk boarding a real bus and using the real passengers as extras. Mind you, not only did he have to board a real bus as the camera operator (depositing his bus fare without taking his eye off the camera's viewfinder), he also had to ask an actor dressed in a full-on mouse suit do the same.

In preproduction, David Birdsell rode the bus several times to map out his route and see how doable his plan was. Deciding early Sunday morning was his best bet, he also realized the logistics of getting his actors off and on the bus required an assistant to help with transportation. Because there was no dialogue in the film, he figured he could augment whatever production sound he captured easily in post; therefore, he decided to forgo a sound person and use the in-camera microphone. As for actors, David knew a guy who he thought would be great as the man. However, anyone could be in the animal suits. It was a real education about friendship when he had to ask a trio of good buddies to spend a sweaty Sunday inside huge animal outfits and "act" in a guerrilla-style production. The guy who played the chicken also had to drive a huge car while wearing a costume in which sight lines were a little scary. Needless to say, there was no special insurance taken out for this shoot.

The filmmaker's two previous short films had debuted at the Sundance Film Festival. When he submitted *Bad Animals*, the DV piece didn't get in. *Bad Animals* did, however, get accepted into the highly prestigious Clermont-Ferrand festival — and it even won a prize. On the basis of that

French award, the flick got invited to show at Cannes during the International Critics Week. For Cannes, Birdsell had to provide a film print. Having shot on tape, his only option was to do a tape-to-film transfer. Because this money was going to come out of his own pocket, David called around to the various companies that do tape-to-film, explaining his short was going to Cannes if he could get a print made. One company agreed to do the work for a discount in exchange for logo placement in the film's end credits. The going price was $350 a minute, and *Bad Animals* runs four and a half minutes. Birdsell talked the transfer company into matching his production cost. After Cannes, the film got picked up by Res Fest, where it went on an extended tour and was issued on one of their DVD collections. It's also played a host of other film festivals, won a few more prizes, and garnered some nice reviews. Not bad for a $2,000 film!

TEN OPINIONS ON DV FILMMAKING

Still not sure whether to DV or not to DV? Perhaps these viewpoints from filmmakers and industry professionals will help sway you.

1

Joel S. Bachar, who founded a screening series called Independent Exposure in 1996 and has shown over eight hundred short films since then:

"As a curator, I consider myself media agnostic. I don't care what the filmmaker shoots on. I can't speak for other curators, but for myself, whatever media you need to use to get the story out there, great!"

2

Our Very First Sex Tape director Amy Talkington:

"DV is getting better and better. Still, the best short films that I've seen — well, except for one at Palm Springs last year — have been on film. If you're going to shoot something on DV, it should be appropriate for the story you're trying to tell. For my most recent short, my friend Matt said, 'I have this idea. It's this couple, they're making a sex tape.' I thought now that's a great reason to shoot on DV! In that instance, it was appropriate, and that's why I used it. *Our Very First Sex Tape* is meant to seem like a sex tape. It's totally choreographed, but it seems like it isn't. Unfortunately, regarding getting programmed at festivals, if you have an intern or a screener popping it in, they can't distinguish it between all the other DV things that really are amateurish and handheld. So I think the DV style is working against us in the festival world."

3

Bad Animals director David Birdsell:

"That DV short was probably the most fun I've had making a film because it didn't involve all the logistical hassles of dealing with a crew. It was more immediate. You have an idea, you tell three or four people, and you do it. You can watch it right away. It's easier to do things on the spur of the moment. You have a lot more flexibility with a smaller crew, less equipment. The main disadvantage is it's not as beautiful as film. So if you're trying to shoot something to capture its beauty, then DV's not going to do it. The quality of video is not quite at the level of film. Maybe it will someday."

4

Rejected director Don Hertzfeldt:

"Film prints will probably never be obsolete — or at least not for a very, very long time. On the contrary, anything you shoot digitally today is much more likely to become obsolete via that format's inevitable upgrades and advances over the next several years."

5

Sales agent and distributor Carol Crowe, President of Apollo Cinema:

"When people shoot digitally, they overshoot. They spend all their time in postproduction because they shot everything in the world. You have to treat it like you're really shooting on film, so you're not shooting a hundred takes of something. Also, so many of them overlight. You have to pay attention to your lighting."

4

Breezeway director George Langworthy:

"I say shoot DV. Because you're always going to be learning a lot making shorts, and DV's just a cheaper paint box. If you shoot 35mm and you're trying something for the very first time, it gets to be pretty expensive. The negative about shooting DV? It doesn't look as good. People don't take it as seriously."

6

John Halacky, acquisitions consultant for IFILM:

"I'm still a film snob, but I have no qualms saying start on video. See what it can do. Twenty takes, who cares? It's video! You're learning! The one thing I have against short filmmakers who do use video is that they're doing it so quick. The one word I have for a lot of them is: tripod. They think, 'Hey, we'll do it handheld, it will look cool, be all *Blair Witch*.' No! It gives people headaches. Shoot on video, great, but try to be as professional as you can."

7

Jennifer Stark, former programmer of the Palm Springs International Festival of Short Films:

"Digital filmmaking allows for a lot of experimentation. It also allows for a lot of mistakes, which I think is really very, very important for filmmakers."

8

Thomas Harris, current programmer of the Palm Springs International Festival of Short Films:

"There is no reason under the sun to shoot celluloid for a short except if (a) you have the money, and (b) it is absolutely something that texturally or artistically is a choice. I think everyone should shoot DV — or HD preferably. The market doesn't care anymore because most of your access is going to be broadcast anyway. You're not going to be seen in local theaters. If I were talking to a feature filmmaker, I would not necessarily tell you to shoot DV; I would probably still encourage you to shoot celluloid because you've got a shot at theatrical exhibition, and the transfer to film is going to cost you a lot of money. But on a short, why not?"

9

Sundance Film Festival senior programmer Trevor Groth:

"There are some really talented filmmakers working in digital video. It's such a logical transition because there is very little revenue generated from shorts, to spend all that money on film to tell these stories doesn't make a lot of sense."

10

Life After Death director Jordan Horowitz:

"If you've got an idea that you know in your heart is solid, then do whatever it takes to get that made. All the countless discussions about film versus video really only amount to one thing: It doesn't matter. The reality is your budget will choose your tools for you. You can make a film with a Fisher Price camera, which people have done successfully, and if it's good, people will watch it."

SHORT RECAP

- Unlike feature filmmakers, directors of short films have a wide variety of formats to choose from.

- There are alternatives to shooting 35mm that you might find more artistically pleasing than DV.

- Don't be a film snob. Shooting on DV is very acceptable in the short film world.

- With DV, you can own and operate your own camera.

- DV is still video. Don't try to fool yourself into thinking it is just as good as film for all projects.

PART II

MAKING YOUR FILM

CHAPTER 7

FROM CONCEPT TO BLUEPRINT

*W*rite *something you can make.*

Everybody has an idea for a short film. Take Lauren Beaumont. Lauren Beaumont came to visit her godmother in Los Angeles and was inspired to write a short. She set her story against the local landmarks she observed during her visit: Ralph's grocery store, Johnny Rockets, Jamba Juice, and Koo Koo Roo. For characters, she decided to include her godmother, Bear, and Bear's friend, Greg. Her stars, however, are five puppies, who get free and roam the streets of Los Angeles. Her title: *Five Puppies on the Run*.

Lauren Beaumont is an organic filmmaker. She also understands the importance of fashioning a visual story that starts fast and strong. She, like many short filmmakers, ran out of steam before she came up with a killer ending for *Five Puppies on the Run*. But give her a break. She was only eight years old at the time. And give her credit: she picked up a pen (more accurately, a purple magic marker) and wrote and storyboarded her short, which is more than most wannabes do.

FIRST THINGS FIRST

Before you even begin writing a short film script, take a few steps back and rethink everything we've covered so far. Your most important consideration is why — why make a short film? The reality is you don't have to make a short — there are more than enough of them already. Remember, you're paying for the privilege of making your film. If you're doing something fairly big budget, you could probably buy a new car instead. Why not better invest your time writing a screenplay? That doesn't cost anything, and you can potentially make a great deal of money as a screenwriter.

To make opening your studio worthwhile, you must be absolutely clear why you are making a short. If your motivation is to learn how to direct, then don't spend a lot of money and shoot on DV. If your goal is to get a career as a Hollywood director, make something that will impress agents and studio executives. When I was producing shorts for the Fox Movie Channel, our "Everything for Free!" modus operandi meant that we ended up shooting a lot of the shorts outside, in existing locations, in daylight. Although this did not bother the filmmakers or anyone at the Fox Movie Channel, when I showed the shorts to an executive from Nickelodeon, she exclaimed in dismay, "All your shorts are shot on street corners!" Luckily, we weren't making shorts with the specific intention of impressing executives from Nickelodeon. Whatever your reason for making a film, don't lose sight of this original motivation.

YOU ARE GOING TO MAKE THIS FILM

"I'm always nervous about can I actually do it, do I have the resources to make it?," claims *Bad Animals* director David Birdsell. "Others write just whatever they want, and then worry about getting it later. Because they're good producer-types, they say, 'I can get fifty extras (or whatever).' For my student short, *Blue City*, I wrote it not knowing if I would ever be able to find streets like I had imagined. And I didn't really. But close enough." If you can't actually get fifty extras or the right streets, you need to rethink your story. When you write a short film script, you're not fancifully sketching your dream house. You're carefully drafting a blueprint for a house you're building yourself.

HOW TO WRITE A GOOD SHORT FILM SCRIPT

Just as a short story can't be constructed like a novel, a short has to be crafted differently than a feature.

- *QUICKLY ESTABLISH YOUR SITUATION.*

Look at Lauren Beaumont's script/storyboard. Her very first image is an establishing shot of the puppies in a cage. We don't need to know their backstory, why they're in a cage, who put them there, when that happened, etc. They're five puppies in a cage, and the film is called *Five Puppies on the Run.* The audience gets the point and is eager to get on with the adventure.

Danny Simon, who back in the day wrote sketch comedy for Sid Caesar, has a good catch phrase to remind writers how important it is to immediately set up the situation and move on. His example is two men standing on a generic street corner. One man says, "Here we are in sunny Spain." Bam! The viewer immediately understands what the situation is and anticipates where the story might be going. Lauren's version of "here we are in sunny Spain" is the shot of the puppies in the cage.

- *START YOUR STORY AS LATE AS POSSIBLE, AND END IT AS SOON AS POSSIBLE.*

"A feature filmmaker has a long time to develop characters and to set the stage," remarks festival programmer Jennifer Stark. "A short filmmaker has to do that with an awful lot of economy. You have to be very focused and very succinct in how you're going to tell your story. Or you'll spend all your time just setting the stage and never actually doing anything."

- *ALWAYS MOVE THE STORY FORWARD.*

Every filmmaker encounters this universal problem: Scenes that you feel are crucial, that you insist get shot, but in editing, you realize those so-called essential scenes are superfluous. Be smart from the start. If a scene (or even a moment) doesn't move the story forward, cut it while your story is still in script form. Your goal should always be to make your plot as tight as possible.

- *ADD A SENSE OF URGENCY.*

If it seems like your story is moving slowly, think of a way to include a sense of urgency. Also known as a "ticking clock." In Lauren Beaumont's case, the adult characters of Bear and Greg should have a reason they have to recapture the puppies by a certain deadline. Or perhaps the puppies must reach a designated location before it's too late.

- *USE DIALOGUE SPARINGLY*

You'll be surprised how many great short films have absolutely no dialogue. I'm not talking about the silent one-reels of Laurel and Hardy. There are many modern day shorts that are dialogue-free. Why? Because shorts are such a visual medium that filmmakers can tell a story through pictures and actions instead of words. And because dialogue reveals the weakness of mediocre actors. Many a line has been spoken during production, but cut in editing in hopes of making the acting look better. "The first short I made was twelve minutes and there's no dialogue," remarks director Mat Fuller. "I know, it sounds like a boring art movie, but it's not. It has a climax. It builds. I've never had anyone tell me it's boring — even people I don't like!"

- *BE BRAVE IN YOUR CHOICES.*

"In a short film, you can do things that a feature-length film just can't pull off," director Mark Borchardt reminds us. "You can ignore the three-act structure. You can break narrative rules. You can break a lot of rules. It's the arena of anything goes!"

- *END YOUR STORY WITH A BANG.*

As you know from seeing countless bad skits on *Saturday Night Live*, it's crucial that you don't let your story limp to an ending just because you don't know exactly how to end it. In the case of Lauren Beaumont's puppies story, she can coast for quite some time with cute puppies racing through recognizable city settings, but for the short to really pay off, she needs a killer ending. In fact, killing the puppies isn't a bad way to cap that plot.

TIME TO GET SERIOUS

Just because you have an idea and fleshed it out doesn't mean you have a script that you should make. Before your studio moves into preproduction, go through your screenplay and be your own harshest critic.

- *IS IT ESSENTIAL?*

Your goal is to have the tightest script possible because — if you're like most short filmmakers — you yourself will have to materialize everything in that script. Is it essential the puppies run by Jamba Juice? Is it really worth your time and effort to get permission from Jamba Juice's corporate office — when in editing you're finally going to realize that running by all those stores doesn't move the story forward fast enough and you'll cut back to only three stores anyway? Be ruthless now when it's all just theoretical.

- *CAN I MAKE IT BETTER?*

Now that everything in your script is essential, you have to assess whether things could be better: more interesting, original, unique, unexpected, stronger, etc. Rather than just having Lauren's generic godmother and godmother's friend in the story, how could the "people" characters become more dynamic? How could they pump up the excitement factor of the puppies' adventure? Re-examine every element in the story to make sure it's the best it possibly can be.

- *DO I SEE IT IN MY HEAD?*

After putting so much thought into your script, it's time to stop thinking and start seeing. Very soon you'll be storyboarding, but right now just stop and "see" your movie. If you're a good organic filmmaker, you probably already have locations and potential cast in mind. Close your eyes and run the movie in your head. Hopefully you're already seeing specific shots, but it's okay if you aren't. After "watching" it, go back and re-read the script. How accurate was your vision? Are there things that you now can cut? Things that you might need to rethink depending on the location? Things you need to clarify on paper so others will see what you see in your head? Now's the time to be specific.

- *CAN I REALLY DO IT?*

Coming up with ideas is easy. Executing them is hard. You might have written a great script that you will indeed make into a short film — once you win the lottery. Right now, you're going to make your script with the money you set aside and no more. Now it's time to do a little pre-preproduction. If Lauren is determined to have Ralph's, Jamba Juice, Johnny Rockets, and Koo Koo Roo, she needs to go visit those exact locations and talk to managers about how to get permission to include their stores in her film. If the corporations turn out to be uncooperative, she'll have to make some hard decisions.

- *WHAT CAN I CHANGE SO I CAN DO IT WITHIN MY BUDGET AND RESOURCES?*

If you don't want to give up, then you'll have to get creative. You could write a script about a man on fire, but unless you know a guy who can do the special effects for free, you really can't make the film. *I'm On Fire*, in fact, is a short that writer/director Ryan Rowe pitched to us at the Fox Movie Channel. My first concern was how to do the extensive special effects of a man on fire — for no money. The director, who is a comedy writer, said, "We'll just get a hobo and light him on fire!" Joking, of course. We did call the fire expert from the Spike Jonze Wax video (which consists of a guy on fire walking down the street in extreme slow motion). Turns out it's outrageously expensive each time you torch a stuntman. In the end, the director found a guy who did special effects on the *Star Trek* series who created the fire on his home computer after work.

- *AM I THE BEST PERSON TO TURN THIS STORY INTO A FILM?*

There's a reason that not all screenwriters are directors. You might have come up with a great story and written the best script that anyone has ever read, but that doesn't mean you're the best person to direct the piece. As the studio, you must honestly decide whether you're going to hire yourself to direct. In the case of little Lauren Beaumont, should she make *Five Puppies on the Run* on her mom's home video camera right now or should she wait until she grows up and goes to film school? No one can make that decision except Lauren. However, I would argue that a preteen would probably make a charmingly naïve film which would most likely get a lot of festival play based on the little girl filmmaker angle.

THINKING IN PICTURES

Okay, you've committed to this script. Let's jump forward to the next step in turning your idea into a blueprint for filmmaking. While the script can contain a general description of what you have in mind, storyboards can make it specific. For example, for the Fox Movie Channel short *I'm on Fire*, the first shot reveals a typical Southern Californian suburban house with a convertible parked in the driveway. The front door flies open. A man, completely engulfed in flames, runs out, gets in his convertible, and drives away. Still on fire.

Do you really need to storyboard this? As with everything in short film-making, you can do whatever you want. But won't it help to know where exactly the car is parked in the driveway, which way the man runs to get into the car, and in which direction the car drives off? Are you going to shoot the scene entirely in a master shot, or are you going to include some close-ups? The director wanted to shoot the entire scene in one unin- terrupted master shot, with the camera observ- ing the action from across the street. Here's the director's storyboard for this first scene:

HOW TO STORYBOARD

Because there are no rules, you can storyboard whichever way works best for you. The ones you see on DVDs or published in books are professional presentational storyboards. Short filmmakers have no need for such flashy artwork (unless you want to!). Some directors use stick figures, some do full-on illustrations. Some use computer programs, some do over-head camera plots. Don't let the fact that you "can't draw" stop you. Some direc- tors go out to the location and take photographs with the appropriate lens- es to previsualize. Even more popular are video storyboards — using a video camera to shoot scenes before you even begin production.

You are expressing visual information for the camera when you storyboard. This is the "composing" part of the director's job. Where is the camera in relation to the actor? What is visible in foreground and in the background? Is it a close-up or a master shot? Don't get trapped into thinking of static shots. Films are moving pictures. That's why arrows are your best friend when storyboarding. Express the action and camera movements with arrows. Don't forget transitions from scene to scene.

Here are a few tips for making storyboarding easier.

- *WHENEVER POSSIBLE, SECURE YOUR LOCATIONS FIRST.*

Having the real location in mind can make storyboarding go much faster. Not having a location shouldn't stop you from doing drawings, but things will definitely change once you have the practical location.

- *TALK THROUGH THE SCRIPT WITH YOUR DIRECTOR OF PHOTOGRAPHY BEFORE BEGINNING TO STORYBOARD.*

More than likely, while you talk, your DP will start making some preliminary sketches or ask you questions that will help clarify shots. Speaking about the pictures in your head before you document them will save you time and frustration.

- *IF YOU HAVE TOO MANY SHOTS TO DRAW, CUT BACK ON YOUR SHOTS.*

If you feel like it's taking forever to storyboard everything you want to shoot, imagine how long it's going to take to actually shoot it. You're clearly being too ambitious. Scale back — now!

- *DON'T FEEL LIKE YOUR STORYBOARDS ARE SACROSANCT.*

They're working documents. Feel free to use them however you want. Some filmmakers cut up the frames and put them on index cards, which can be shuffled around to make shot lists.

INSIDER INFORMATION ON THE IMPORTANCE OF STORYBOARDING

In addition to being a talented short filmmaker, Robbie Consing is a storyboard artist who has worked on major films such as *Minority Report* and *Mission Impossible 2.* "If you don't storyboard your short film or have someone do it for you, you should be shot," Robbie proclaims. "You really should not even be allowed to do a short! Because this is your first film. You should not assume you know how to control a shot without having to have it already illustrated. Storyboarding forces you to think about your own movie. If you don't, if you don't come prepared, if you say 'I'll just tell them what to do on that day and we'll find it,' that's not exactly fair to your crew. Whatever inspiration you think you're going to get is going to kill them and you.

"Storyboarding is the way to get everyone started. The DP has to understand what you're talking about, and the actors have to know where they're blocking. If they don't know where they are going to be because you didn't take time to figure it out (especially since you're the one making up the schedule), what possible complaint can you have when things fall apart, organizational-wise? Storyboards are a shot list, first and foremost. The same way your script should be. If you're shooting junk, you're not going to have anything to cut when it comes to editing. Or too much to cut. With storyboarding, you can tell if your stuff is going to cut together.

"When it comes to directing, the only homework you really have as a short filmmaker (besides paying the tab) is storyboarding, rehearsing, and block-ing. Because let's face it, what possible excuse do you have for not being pre-pared on your own set when all the elements, all the molecules, are all you?"

SHORT RECAP

- A good story is everything.

- Be ruthless about retooling your story and rewriting your script until every moment is the best it can possibly be.

- Before you sign off on your script, visualize the movie in your head.

- You don't have to be able to draw well to storyboard. Stick figures are perfectly fine.

- Don't be afraid to make changes as your start visualizing your story. Story-boarding should help you realize where you can cut back on your script.

CHAPTER 8

BUDGETING:
EVERYTHING FOR FREE

Only spend money when you must.

Budgeting is easy for short filmmakers who subscribe to the "Everything for Free! Everyone Works for Free!" mandate. We also know what our final production budget will be because we work backward from the amount of money we can spend — our "in the can" fund. Before we seriously dig into budgeting, we first have to break down the script to see what exactly we're going to be getting for free.

THINKING IN TERMS OF BIG TICKET ITEMS

Big ticket items traditionally refer to expensive items. Since in theory we are not paying for anything, we define the term slightly differently. In the "beg, borrow, and steal" world, big ticket items are things you will not compromise on because you feel they are crucial to the success of your film — so crucial you may break your "Everything for Free!" rule to get them.

Guess what the two most essential big ticket items should be for every short film. Here's a clue: If they're sub par, they'll destroy your film. Yes, it's acting and sound. We'll discuss the pros and cons of hiring Screen Actors Guild talent in Chapter 9, but the reason why so many short filmmakers do sign with the Guild is they feel it's worth all the hassles SAG contracts entail to get the best actors they can. As for sound, sometimes you have to pay for good location sound. Any penny you try to save during production will cost you pounds of aggravation in post.

The third essential big ticket item tends to be "shooting on film." Ultimately, if you feel it's crucial your flick be shot on film but you can't get the necessary camera and stock for free, you must decide how much you are willing to compromise or to pay to make it happen. Perhaps you can convince yourself to settle on the less expensive 16mm.

If you can't achieve your crucial big ticket items, postpone production until you can. With *He Had a Hat*, the filmmaker's inability to get special effects for free killed the project. *I'm on Fire* would have been history if the director hadn't found someone to create fire effects on his home computer. For *Five Puppies on the Run*, Jamba Juice and all the other stores aren't essential. Without the puppies, though, you don't have a film.

Every big ticket item is a big decision. One of our Fox Movie Channel shorts called *Phil Touches Flo* featured a pug (Flo). My first question to the director: "Does it have to be a pug?" Yes, he felt quite firmly that the whole story wouldn't work without a pug. We lucked out and found the pug who had been in *Men in Black*. The dog was very well trained, and it saved us a lot of time on set having a pro. However, because there was a crucial scene in the film where the dog had to run on its own and turn a corner, there had to be two trainers on set — each of whom had to be paid. Let's just say that dog turned out to be a really big ticket item. But if you asked the director, he'd say it was worth every penny.

MAKING A BUDGET

Unlike a feature, you don't need to do a big fancy budget for your little film. A simple item-by-item listing in Excel will do fine. Most things are for free anyway! If you're dealing with SAG or an insurance agency, they will request that you submit your budget, but they're used to seeing informal ones from short filmmakers, so don't think you have to fancy it up for them.

The most crucial thing about budgeting is to remember the amount you promised yourself you wouldn't spend more than. If your budget before production is scarily close to that number, you're in trouble because production always end up costing more than you expect. You need to spend more time trying to get everything for free so you won't blow your budget.

HOW MUCH FOR A CHICKEN SUIT?

As a case study, let's breakdown the *Bad Animals* film discussed in Chapter 6.

CAST (LEADS):
- Man
- Chicken
- Mouse
- Bear

CAST (EXTRAS/ATMOSPHERE):
- People on the bus
- People on the street

WARDROBE:
- Man's casual work clothes
- Chicken suit
- Bear suit
- Mouse suit

LOCATIONS:
- Street w/ bus stop
- Bus
- Street

PROPS:
- Bus fare
- Chloroform
- Rag for chloroform

VEHICLES:
- Bus
- Chicken's car (convertible to accommodate chicken costume height)

CREW:
- Camera operator
- (No sound, no lighting)
- Assistant to transport actors/take behind-the-scenes photos

EQUIPMENT:
- Camera — a borrowed Canon Optura (the same style of mini-DV camera used to shoot *405*)

- DV tapes — 2 (free from production company)
- Camera mount (for car shots)

What are the big ticket items? The obvious one is the bus. However, the director knew he was going to guerrilla that. For him, the costumes were the most crucial thing. He dragged his friend around from costume shop to costume shop until he found the right chicken outfit. Unfortunately, at the "chicken" shop, he couldn't find another outfit he liked, so he continued going to wardrobe houses until he found the other animal outfits. At the second house, he used the price paid for the chicken costume as his benchmark, talking all the houses into matching it.

Here is how the director accounted for his $1,000 production budget.

PRODUCTION COSTS:

ACTORS (4) + CREW ASSISTANT (1): 5 X $50 = $250
[Because he did have a grand to spend, the director paid everyone who worked on the film. If you're going to break the "Everyone Works for Free!" rule, pay everyone the same amount as a flat fee to avoid any complications.]

DIRECTOR: $100
[He allowed himself 10% of the budget as a fee. Taking a percentage of the budget is always a good strategy if you're asked to name your fee.]

FOOD: $80
[Since it was a one-day shoot, no catering was necessary. The director took everyone out to lunch and picked up the tab.]

COSTUMES (RENTAL): 3 X $100 = $300
[Thus it was established that a hundred bucks will cover a weekend rental charge for a chicken outfit.]

COSTUMES (DRY CLEANING): $25
[The animal outfits didn't require laundering, but the actor playing the man wore his own work clothes, which did get taken to the dry cleaners.]

CAR (WEEKEND RENTAL): $150

[The original thought was just to borrow a friend's car, but the chicken head was too large to fit inside a traditional car. Once again the director decided to spend some dough rather than seeking out a free car. Since he was paying for it, he rented the largest car possible for $150. If he had tried to get it free, he would have done the "Want to be in pictures?" note under the windshields in parking lots technique. Or he could have asked the car rental place if they'd lend it to him for free if he cut the short down into a promotional piece/spec commercial for them featuring the car, which they could play on their web site or use as a local cable ad. The car rental company would be extremely foolish to pass up an offer to get a free commercial made for them.]

PROPS: $5

[Yes, he paid five bucks for a chloroform-looking bottle and rag. Robert Rodriguez would not approve!]

BUS FARE: $30

[This amount included checking out the possible bus routes during pre-production]

CAMERA: FREE

[You can always find someone's camera to borrow. In this case, having such a small mobile camera allowed the director to mount the camera all over the chicken's convertible, giving the film an invaluable sense of motion.]

TAPE: FREE

[Finally, here's something done in "beg, borrow, and steal" style!]

CAMERA CAR MOUNT (RENTAL): $15

[Best $15 ever spent!]

LENS (RENTAL): $30

[If you do shoot mini-DV, being able to add a lens gives you more options.]

BEHIND-THE-SCENES STILL CAMERA FILM & PROCESSING: $15

[The photos you see throughout this guide were paid for by that fifteen bucks. Of course, if they had taken digital stills, this budget could have been $15 less.]

POST COSTS:

EDITING: FREE
[Because the filmmaker is also a professional editor, he edited the film himself on a borrowed system. Although he added some sound effects in post, he chose not to include any music.]

MASTER TAPE: FREE
[Beg, borrow, and steal!]

TOTAL COST: $1,000

HOW MUCH FOR A PUG?

In comparison to the one-day, guerilla-style, mini-DV *Bad Animals* shoot, here's an "Everything for Free! Everyone Works for Free!" version of the budget for Fox Movie Channel short *Phil Touches Flo*, the "pug" movie. The story for the short can be summed up in four sentences: Flo is a dog. Flo's owner doesn't like people touching Flo. Flo's owner is not a nice man. Phil touches Flo. Inspired by the strange outcropping of two palm trees in an otherwise barren industrial section of downtown Los Angeles, the short takes place entirely on that street, where we shot for two days, with permits and a big crew, on 35mm. As we go through the budget, it will become immediately obvious what the two big ticket items were. By the way, we'll cover what all these crew people do in Chapter 10 and what the postproduction steps are in Chapter 12.

PRODUCER'S UNIT
PRODUCER: $0

[You'll notice the only people who get paid in this "Everyone Works for Free!" budget are the ones we can't get away with not paying, i.e. the dog trainers and the police.]

DIRECTION
DIRECTOR: $0

CAST/CASTING:
3 ACTORS x 2 DAYS: $0
DOG ($250) x 2 DAYS = $500
[The dog had a flat rate, but the trainers went into overtime after eight hours.]
DOG TRAINERS ($219.20) x 2 TRAINERS X 2 DAYS = $877
CASTING DIRECTOR = $0

TOTAL ABOVE THE LINE = $1,377

PRODUCTION STAFF
PRODUCTION MANAGER = $0
1ST ASSISTANT DIRECTOR = $0
2ND ASSISTANT DIRECTOR = $0
SCRIPT SUPERVISOR = $0
POLAROID FOR SCRIPT SUPERVISOR = $25
[How old-fashioned is taking Polaroids! Use digital cameras instead of Polaroid whenever you can. In general, several departments will need to take photographs to keep continuity: script supervisor, wardrobe, make-up/hair, and art department. Try to sell them all on the glory of digital photographs.]

PRODUCTION ASSISTANTS X 4 = $0
OFFICE SUPPLIES (XEROXING @ KINKOS) = $19
[Hard to beg from Kinko's! Because our production was very paper-oriented, we were always making xeroxes on location.]

SET OPERATIONS
KEY GRIP: $0
GRIPS (DOLLY + 3) = $0
GRIP TRUCK/EQUIPMENT RENTAL = $500
[In this case, the reason we got a great grip is we agreed to rent his truck full of equipment. You can do this much cheaper! However, expendables were covered in this flat fee. Expendables, as you will discover, are a hidden

cost. Each crew member who uses their own supplies will ask you to give them a kit fee to cover their out-of-pocket expenses. It's true, they are using material that will have to be replaced, so it's hard to argue with them.]
GRIP EXPENDABLES = $0
CATERING (40 PEOPLE X 2 DAYS X $11.50,
PLUS EXTRA MISC. CHARGES) = $943
[Food is always where the bulk of your money goes during production. If you have the time, you can try to make everything yourself ahead of time, but you don't want to be like a team of directors I know, one of whom had to step off set to make the peanut butter and jelly sandwiches for everyone.]
SECOND MEAL (PIZZA) = $48
[We only had to do second meal once, but you should have a little extra tucked away for a pizza run should the shoot day extend into night.]
CRAFT SERVICE = $238
[This is a crazy amount for craft service!]
RUNNER'S MILEAGE/GAS = $25
[You can refuse to reimburse for gas/mileage, but if you do, make sure everyone understands this up front so there's no misunderstanding later.]
LOSS & DAMAGE = $0

SET DECORATING & PROPERTY
ART DIRECTOR (NONE)
[The organic location meant we didn't need any art direction.]
PROPS:
DOG TAG + ENGRAVING = $5
[It was only $5, but this probably could have been begged by promising the engraver a thanks or a logo in the credits.]
STUN GUN = $21
[Bought from a pawn shop, and returned after the shoot. Try to return as many things as possible after you know you definitely won't need to do any reshoots.]
BATTERIES FOR STUN GUN = $4
[Batteries will kill you every time.]

WARDROBE
COSTUME DESIGNER = $0
WARDROBE PURCHASES/RENTAL = $0
DRY CLEANING = $30
[If actors wear their own clothes, it's common practice to offer to pick up the

dry cleaning costs. If you buy new clothes from department stores and plan on returning them when the shoot's done, don't clip the tags.]

MAKEUP & HAIR
MAKEUP ARTIST = $0
KIT FEE ($25) X 2 DAYS = $50
[I don't know why we paid such a high kit fee because we only had three men and a dog in the cast.]

LIGHTING
GAFFER (NONE)
[Shooting outdoors in sunshine means natural lighting, so no electricity or special lighting was necessary. We did have some bounce boards, which grips manned.]
ELECTRICIAN (NONE)
SWING GRIP/ELECTRIC (NONE)
GENERATOR RENTAL (NONE)
EQUIPMENT RENTAL/PURCHASES (NONE)
LOSS & DAMAGE (NONE)

CAMERA
DIRECTOR OF PHOTOGRAPHY = $0
1ST ASSISTANT CAMERAPERSON = $0
2ND ASSISTANT CAMERAPERSON = $0
LOADER = $0
STILL PHOTOGRAPHER (PUBLICITY) = $0
[Usually even if you have a friend do it, you should cover the costs of the film, processing, and prints.]
CAMERA TRUCK RENTAL = $200
[You can definitely get this cheaper.]
GAS FOR TRUCK = $36
[Our location was very close.]
CAMERA RENTALS (FREE 35MM CAMERA) = $0
[The trick to getting a free camera is to have your director of photography pull some strings. You will, however, need insurance. Also some camera rental houses might require a deposit, which they'll refund when you bring everything back.]
CAMERA EXPENDABLES = $25
[A kit fee to one of the assistant camerapeople for using their supplies.]

DOLLY = $300
[You should be able to get a free dolly if you try. We didn't.]

SOUND
SOUND MIXER = $0
BOOM OPERATOR = $0
SOUND EQUIPMENT RENTAL ($250) X 2 DAYS = $500
["Everyone Works for Free!" except those who charge you to use their equipment. Consider the sound equipment rental a really big kit fee.]
SOUND EXPENDABLES (DAT/BATTERIES) = $30
[Even with that huge rental, the sound engineer charged for expendables. Batteries again!]
WALKIE-TALKIES X 10 = $46
[Make sure you have a sign-out sheet for walkies to keep track of who has one and who returns theirs. Almost every shoot seems to have one go missing. Walkie-talkies are very, very expensive to replace.]

LOCATION
PERMITS:
[Since we were shooting in downtown Los Angeles, we had to get a permit from the city. The permit office decides what will be required. In our case, not only did we have the permit, spot check, and postings fees, we had to hire two police officers, who got paid overtime after eight hours. Notice how the location, the second big ticket item we're willing to spend money on, is getting out of control.]
LA CITY PERMIT = $385
SPOT CHECK FEE = $85
POSTING = $72
LOCATION CLEANING (WATER TRUCK/TRASH PICK UP) = $455
[The "free location" was so filthy that we were seriously worried it might be a health hazard for the actors and crew to spend two days there. We ended up having to hire two different private companies to hose down the street and sidewalk, and then do trash removal.]
SITE RENTAL = $0
[Ha! Our "free" site turned out to be pretty expensive. However, the fact that it came pre-art directed with amazing graffiti should always be taken into account. Another plus: because the street was deserted, we had no problems with neighbors, traffic, or noise.]

LOCATION SUPPLIES (SIGNS) = $19
POLICE X 2 X 2 DAYS = $1,107
DAMAGES = $0
MISC. (PHOTOGRAPHS OF SITE FOR STORYBOARDS) = $35

PRODUCTION FILM & LAB
NEGATIVE RAW STOCK:
STOCK 5293 400' X 2 = $0
STOCK 5293 1000' X 4 = $0
[Free film! The filmmaker was given a ten-to-one shooting ratio, which means for a five-minute long film he should have shot fifty minutes worth of film (35mm runs ninety feet a minute). However, according to the lab reports, somehow he shot 7,550 feet of film. It's possible there were extra cans of film that we didn't record in the budget because film stock was free. By the way, ten-to-one is too generous of a shooting ratio, even with free film.]
DEVELOPING:
DEVELOP COLOR NEG X 7,550' = $0
[Free processing! In general, processing isn't a large cost if your footage count is low]
PREP FOR TELECINE = $0
TELECINE X 4 HOURS = $0
[All that footage means many hours were spent in telecine, laying down the footage to video. Even if telecine is free, the tape stock isn't. Although they don't use the word expendables in post, that's basically what it is.]
DIGIBETA STOCK:
60 MINUTES X 1 = $215
30 MINUTES X 1 = $160
TOTAL PRODUCTION = $5578

EDITING
EDITOR = $0
EDITING SYSTEM = $0
NEGATIVE CUT = $745

MUSIC
COMPOSER = $0

POSTPRODUCTION SOUND
SOUND EFFECTS/FOLEY STUDIO = $0

DAT + DA-88 TAPES = $40
OPTICAL TRACK (680') = $359
[Didn't get the optical track for free.]

TITLES
TITLES & OPTICALS = $0

LAB
ANSWER PRINT = $0
RELEASE PRINTS = $0

INSURANCE
INSURANCE = $0
[We did have insurance, but under the Fox corporate policy.]

TOTAL POST = $1144

TOTAL COSTS = $8099

Note: The film runs a little over seven minutes, so with everyone working for free and most everything regarding shooting on film for free, this budget did come out in the "budget $1,000 per minute" range. This budget, however, is fudged. At the Fox Movie Channel, we did pay everyone who worked on the films. And we did pay full rate for a few things that we should have gotten for free. In reality, the film cost a little more than twenty thousand. But that's another story.

SHORT RECAP

- Break down your script to see what you need to make your film.

- Evaluate what you can get for free.

- Put your effort into securing necessary big ticket items. Don't compromise on these most essential elements.

- If you want to pay people, pay every person on the crew the same amount.

- Even with the cheapest shoot, you'll have to pay for food and "expendables."

CHAPTER 9

SAG: FRIEND OR FOE

***You** might not need Screen Actors Guild talent. But if you do, do it right.*

If you read no other chapter in this book but this one, you'll be miles ahead of the game. Because the two biggest sandtraps in short filmmaking involve actors. One is bad acting, which, along with bad sound, is the artistic downfall of many a potentially good short film. The second hazard is signing a contract with the Screen Actors Guild without really understanding all that it entails. Before we get tangled up in SAG issues, let's look big picture when it comes to working with actors.

"Often I get so caught up in the logistics and camera angles and lighting and time schedule that I always forget or give virtually no attention to the most important element of all: the acting," reveals filmmaker Jordan Horowitz. "People will forgive almost everything but bad acting. That's what everyone watching the film will use to size up your skill as a director. I don't care how fancy you are with a camera; if your actors suck, then so do you."

HOW TO AVOID BAD ACTING
Hire good actors. Direct them well.

HOW TO HIRE GOOD ACTORS
Finding your actors is the fun part of preproduction. Think of it as a shopping spree that won't cost you a penny. You may be thinking of casting yourself or friends, and that can be a very good option. But if you want to hire people you don't know to portray the characters in your piece, there are many ways of finding them.

- *WATCH SHORTS AND FEATURE FILMS MADE BY FILMMAKERS IN YOUR TOWN.*

Are there any actors that interest you? Track them down via the filmmakers. This is a wonderful way of shopping for actors, because not only do you see how they look on film, you can get the real skinny from their previous director on what it's like to work with them.

- *RUN AN AD AND THEN HOLD A CASTING SESSION.*

Ah, the casting session. Casting can be a lot of fun because it can open your eyes to an entire range of possibilities. Perhaps you always pictured a small man in a role that really comes alive when portrayed by a fat man. Not only will you benefit from seeing different people, auditions are a great opportunity to polish your "working with actors" directing skills. Ask actors to tackle the material in different manners. Can they stretch their interpretation? Can they give you what you want? Better to know now rather than on the set if someone is a one-trick pony. You'll also get a sense if this is an actor that will take up a lot of your time on set with needy behavior.

Casting sessions are also a wonderful opportunity to test out your material. Are lines falling flat no matter who says them? Are actors telling you they don't understand what the scene is about or why their character acts a certain way? You need to go back and fix the script.

CASTING STARS

Believe it or not, it's relatively easy to cast stars in your short. It helps if you know them. Grant Heslov got George Clooney to appear in his thirty-minute romantic comedy, *Waiting for Woody*. Of course, Grant happens to be one of George's best buds. But you don't have to have already shared a beer or two with Clooney to get him to be in your movie. All you have to do is call the Screen Actors Guild, ask them to tell you the star's agent, call the agent, and ask that your project be considered.

Why should George Clooney's agent take your call? Three reasons. Because you're going to be the next Spike Jonze, and George Clooney likes to work with on-the-cusp, extremely creative filmmakers. Because everyone knows shorts are where the really adventurous filmmaking takes place. And because you've got a project that is one hundred times more exciting than most of the run-of-the-mill features he's offered.

Mat Fuller had a former pop star in his film: Danny Wood from New Kids on the Block. "I don't have this cool story about how I sent a script to his agent or anything," says Fuller. "When we were casting *Deveria*, the production coordinator on my film knew Danny. She's from

Miami, and he was her neighbor. She asked if I would be interested in using him because he wanted stuff for his reel. That's the key. It sounds stupid, but I think the easiest way to get someone who has any kind of name is to get a guy who is trying to transition from TV to film. Danny did it for free. Find a guy who's looking for stuff for his reel. That's what I gave Danny. He got an agent out of it, so he was happy with me. And I was a little bit lucky with the timing in terms of the New Kids thing. My short came out at the time that Mark Wahlberg had a big movie coming out, Donnie Wahlberg was on *Band of Brothers*, and Danny Wood had just done a short! So there was some value there."

There are additional values to having a name in your film. "Mark Wahlberg saw my film. He hasn't asked me to do his movies yet," laughs Mat, "but having Danny in the film got me that exposure. And the cool thing is — on top of that, forget the good it does your movie — I know Danny now. He has a CD coming out, and I get first pitch on his video."

So "name" actors of all levels are attainable. But do you want them?

PROS OF HIRING NAME ACTORS

- They're much better actors than your Uncle Charlie.

- The other actors' performances will rise to a higher level as a result of working with a better "player."

- People will be impressed that you have someone they've heard of in your little movie.

- The name actor could potentially hire you in the future.

- Your work gets shown to their high-powered friends in the industry.

CONS OF HIRING NAME ACTORS

- They're used to professional productions. Stars don't understand the realities of no-budget filmmaking. Let's just say they're not too happy about public restrooms doubling as dressing rooms.

- They're used to unlimited takes. They're looking at your film as a chance to stretch as actors, and they'll want to experiment with their performance. You, on the other hand, have limited film stock and a busy day to get through. Neither of you will be happy with the results.

- You will be intimidated. They do have much more experience than you do and have worked with the best. The last thing you need is to feel inferior on your own set.

- If you get George Clooney, you'll discover it will be hard to get people to focus on your contributions when all they'll want to talk about is the former ER hunk.

- You're a victim of their schedule. And stars have very busy and unpredictable lives. You may be prepared to start filming on Saturday, but if they get a last minute invitation to fly to Aspen for the weekend, they'll expect you to wait for them to return. Or if they have to leave early to attend a premiere, you'll have to shoot around them. In the balance of power, they're doing you a favor by being in your film.

CASTING FRIENDS

Why ask strangers to act in your project when the perfect person to portray your character might be right under your nose?

Robbie Consing decided to cast his good friend Guy Dyas as one of the two leads in his Fox Movie Channel short, *Beeker's Crossing*. He knew Guy had the right look for the part and wrote the role with Guy in mind. The only problem: Guy is not an actor. "Writing the short film," Robbie muses, "when you visualize somebody who you think might be right, you corner yourself. Which, of course, is good when you're writing because the more corners you have, the easier is it to let things flow out. It gives you more inspiration to do certain things. Having the person be a friend whose personality and look are perfect, the advantages are plentiful. Number one, he's a good friend of mine. I know what his strengths and weaknesses are. Number two, he won't mind the long hours — which any filmmaker will definitely appreciate! Number three (and this is very crucial), you can be honest with him. And friends usually understand what their limits are. Now if you have friends who are dying to be actors and they're not very good actors, that can be incredibly hellish. What I would say to anyone who ever wants to roll film, do not ever, ever, ever promise parts to friends who are dying to act until they either audition or do a tape and see for themselves whether they are right for the role. Because you will know right then and there if they are. And I would never ever, ever again promise a friend a role unless I taped them first. Because my friend was more terrified about it than I was, I later found out."

Would he recommend hiring non-actors? "It just depends on what kind of short it is," replies Robbie, "what characters they are playing, and how much is it about their look or their presence. Guy has enough charisma to power any ten short films. Can he act? I think he can, and I think I got a great performance out of him."

Filmmaker Mark Borchardt also hires non-pros. "Sometimes a non-actor can bring charisma to screen that an actor cannot," says Borchardt, "because an actor is a trained professional with a certain flow of instinct bred through instruction in the craft, where a non-actor can bring a sense of aliveness and spontaneity because that's all he knows. It can be quite charming on screen. Working with professional actors, it's far more technically easy to deal with them because they understand about hitting marks and this and that. Whereas people off the street who are quite adept at adapting, they immediately get it, too. But real actors have a sense of shedding self-awareness so they're acting as a job where people off the street might obviously overact, trying to figure out how to act. I tell anyone who is nervous about acting, 'Don't act, man. Be.'"

CASTING YOURSELF

"It's easy to get too overwhelmed if you want to be in it as well as direct it," advises Tara Vernerso, who played the lead in one of her experimental films. "Also you don't have the same vision when you're in it as when you're a voyeur, looking at the action from the outside and directing it. If you're in your short for an artistic reason beyond vanity, then you might consider it. But if you are directing just to pursue your acting career, perhaps you should hire a director. And if you are directing it only because you can't find a director to do it, you might want to reevaluate your acting ability!"

TEN TIPS FOR GETTING GREAT PERFORMANCES

1

REHEARSE.

Work as much as you can with your actors in preproduction. Recording your rehearsals on video is also highly recommended.

2

DON'T GET OVERWHELMED BY THE MYRIAD OF DETAILS A DIRECTOR IS SUPPOSED TO SUPERVISE ON SET.

Remember that it's the actors' performances that will make your film. Pay attention to the on-screen drama, not the petty behind-the-scenes dramas.

3

PLAY TO YOUR ACTORS' STRENGTH.

Don't ask an inexperienced cast member to reach outside of their natural way of doing things, where they are forced to "perform."

4

LESS IS MORE.

The camera catches more than your naked eye. A deadpan performance can read on film as something real and emotionally deep, whereas theatrical-style acting will seem too big and unnatural.

5

SHOOT ACTORS LISTENING OR REACTING.

Great actors always swear that the secret to acting is listening. During each take, make sure your actors are listening to each other rather than just waiting to deliver their own lines. During editing, you're going to want to be able to cutaway from the actor speaking to show others reacting — especially if you have an actor delivering a large chunk of dialogue.

6

DON'T LET ACTORS BURN THROUGH TAPE (OR FILM) DOING DIFFERENT TAKES.

Get what you need, then move on.

7

WHEN POSSIBLE, HAVE THE ACTORS SPEAK AT A QUICK PACE.

Movies move faster than real life. If you don't want scenes to drag, your direction to sluggish actors should be, "Once more, only faster."

8

RECORD WILD TRACK LINES OF DIALOGUE ON THE SET.

If you don't think you'll be able to do decent ADR (automatic dialogue replacing, or looping) in post, consider doing a down and dirty version on set. While rolling sound only, let the actors try different ways of delivering their dialogue. You never know what you'll need during editing, and it's nice to have some options at your fingertips.

9

IF YOU CAN AVOID IT, DON'T HAVE CHARACTERS TALK ON THE PHONE.

Actors are better and scenes more dynamic when the characters interact face to face.

10

WITH KIDS OR ANIMALS, SHOOT THE REHEARSAL.

Understand that they both have limited attention spans. And when they're tired, you might as well just call it a day and send everyone home.

LET'S TALK ABOUT PAPERWORK

Anyone who appears on camera must sign a personal depiction release. You could get a lawyer to draw up a document for you, or you could just buy a pad of inexpensive generic release forms from Enterprise Printers and Stationers (*www.enterpriseprinters.com*). If the film stars your best friend, you might be tempted to skip the paperwork. Don't. Because when you later try to sell your film, no potential distributor will touch it if you don't have all your actor releases signed. You can always go back to your stars after the fact and get them to sign a release, but it's easier to do it during production when you have guaranteed access to everyone.

AND NOW LET'S TALK ABOUT SAG

Up until this point, you've controlled everything about your film. When you sign with the Screen Actors Guild, you give up a huge part of that control. Now you are a SAG signature company, and you must play by their rules. The thing you have to remember about SAG is that you're going to be dealing with them for the rest of your professional life, so you don't want to get on their bad side. The good news is they recognize you are indeed a studio just like a major studio, and you are treated just like any other SAG production. The bad news is SAG demands you to play the game just like the big boys do, and that means professional working conditions, hours, paperwork, and payments.

The many things they require you to be professional about include:

• *COPYRIGHT REGISTRATION.*
SAG demands you to register your film script with the copyright office — not for your protection, but for theirs. The Guild recognizes that you are starting to build a property that has value, and that value starts with the copyright.

• *WORKERS' COMPENSATION*
You must prove to the Guild that your actors will be insured. This is, in fact, a good thing for everyone's protection. However, if you weren't planning on getting insurance, you are now.

• *SAG WORKING CONDITIONS, PAPERWORK, AND HOURS.*
Even though you're not paying your actors up front when you defer salary by doing a SAG low budget or experimental film agreement, you are

agreeing to run your set in compliance with all of SAG's rules and regulations. Again, this is a good thing for everyone involved, but it means someone else is dictating how you run your show.

- *THERE IS NO FREE LUNCH.*

Depending on the agreement you sign, you may get away with not paying your actors any money up front. But you will have to pay them immediately and in full if your short starts to make money. This is where many films get caught in a trap. Because the money a short film can generate from licensing opportunities is rarely enough to pay off all SAG fees, consequently filmmakers have to turn down low offers — because of their SAG agreement.

"This is where I made a mistake: I didn't pay my actors up front," shares *White Face* director Brian McDonald. "I went under the experimental agreement. Under the experimental agreement, I don't have to pay the actors unless the film makes money. Everyone knows shorts don't make money, so you don't have to worry about that. So I didn't worry about it. Then the film started to make money, and I owed my actors all this money. From now on, I'll always assume my films are going to make a million dollars and pay my actors the lower rate up front. Because otherwise you end up screwing yourself."

Why have that massive IOU hanging over your head? The simple answer is you want great actors because bad acting is the death of most shorts.

- *DON'T FORGET ABOUT SAG-PRODUCERS PENSION AND HEALTH PLANS AND ROYALTIES.*

The SAG headaches just keep on coming.

SAG IS NOT YOUR FRIEND

Don't be afraid of dealing with SAG. The reps are wonderful people who do understand that you are a talented director who is going far. They also understand you're a novice learning the ropes of film production. They want to help you do everything right (right, according to SAG, that is).

But make no mistake. SAG is very up front about whose side they're on: their members, the actors. SAG is not your guild — it's the actors' guild.

IF YOU DO GO THE SAG ROUTE

You must begin conversations with SAG at least a month before you plan to begin shooting in order to do your paperwork in the proper amount of time. There are several types of agreements. If you are a student currently enrolled in film school, you may do a student contract in which the actors can defer their entire salary. You will need to produce a letter from your instructor confirming that you are indeed enrolled in a filmmaking class and that you are making the film as part of the course. If you're not a student production, then you'll qualify for one of the low budget or experimental agreements. A SAG rep will explain all of the differences and help you select the plan that works best for you.

When you first begin dealing with SAG, you will have to submit to the representative assigned to your project a full packet of information including the following material:

- *YOUR SCREENPLAY AS YOU PLAN TO SHOOT IT.*

SAG will not accept first drafts or treatments. Problem areas your rep will be looking for include hazardous situations or nudity.

- *A COPY OF YOUR ACTUAL BUDGET, INCLUDING ANY PAYMENTS YOU PLAN TO DEFER.*

For features, a professionally prepared budget is expected. With a short, you can get away with a relatively informal list of categories and costs. Be very liberal with your use of "∅" in filling out how much you are paying for people and things. SAG wants to make sure that everyone else isn't getting paid while you ask the actors to defer payment. Your rep will, however, look at the bottom line to help you decide which of their SAG agreements will work best for you.

- *A LETTER OF INTENT CONTAINING THE FOLLOWING INFORMATION:*

a) Title of your short film.

b) The date you plan to begin production (i.e., start date). Make sure this is indeed at least 30 days from the day you meet with your rep.

c) Your estimated wrap date. It's okay if your wrap date is the same as your start date if you're doing a one-day shoot.

d) The total shoot days.

e) What format you plan to shoot on (DV, 35mm, etc.).

f) The estimated total running time of your film when edited. Give this number in minutes (e.g., 10 minutes).

g) A summation of your budget.

h) The total number of speaking roles.

i) An estimated number of SAG performers vs. non-SAG.

Once you begin the process, the Guild will supply you with production paperwork including sample performers' contracts, cast list information, and daily production time report forms. If you are negligent, delinquent, or don't comply with your production paperwork, SAG can fine you.

"Working with SAG seems overwhelming, seems like a hassle," remarks filmmaker Amy Talkington. "The best thing is not to be afraid of them. You need to call them, talk to them, and they generally will work with you. But if you cross them, it's a mistake that will come back and haunt you for the rest of your life."

SHORT RECAP

- The Screen Actors Guild is a professional organization that expects you to be professional.

- To be a SAG signatory, you have to play by their rules.

- Look at dealing with SAG on your short as a learning opportunity so when you make your feature you'll already be a pro at SAG rules and regulations.

- Do not lie to SAG. This is an organization you will be dealing with for the rest of your filmmaking career, and you do not want to be on their bad side.

- If you defer payment to your actors and then get an offer to commercially exhibit your film which will not cover your SAG fees, you might not be able to take the offer. Talk to your SAG rep ahead of time about the repercussions of deferring payment.

CHAPTER 10

ESSENTIAL PEOPLE AND PAPERWORK

Whether your production consists of five or fifty people, you need to be organized.

When it comes to deciding how you're going to run your production, the concept of "you are the studio" comes heavily into play. You can have a completely anarchistic/guerilla attitude, not bothering with talent releases, location permission forms, workers' comp, or insurance of any kind. You can incorporate television shows taped off TV and include any music you want without asking for permission. You can do whatever you want because no one can stop you — you're the boss.

This route certainly allows complete creative freedom. It also makes it impossible to do anything with your film once you decide to enter "the real world." If you don't have the rights to the material contained within your film, cable channels, DVD companies, and even Internet sites won't touch your film with a ten foot pole.

In contrast, maybe you are the kind of studio that is very meticulous, dotting all your i's and crossing all your t's. You'll file a copyright on your script and the resulting film, create production reports, get signed releases from everyone involved, get insurance, pay for permits, negotiate music rights or hire a local band to compose music in a work-for-hire situation.

You might find that playing it straight might force you to artistically compromise your film. For example, you're not going to be able to include that Rolling Stones song you dreamed of. But if you plan on making features, it's great training to do things the way "real" filmmakers do. And most importantly, if you've done everything right and have no clearance issues with your final work, you can commercially exhibit your film. Translation: make money off it.

Those two models, of course, are the extremes. You will find a happy balance that works for you. Having produced shorts for the Fox Movie Channel, I come from the get-a-permit, get-permission school of filmmaking. I know a lot of filmmakers who never permit locations and have never been busted. If you do get in trouble, you just claim to be a dumb short filmmaker who doesn't know better. Even people in authority know that shorts are a learning experience for everyone and that there's no money involved, so most will cut you some slack.

PAPERWORK IS SEXY
Okay, it's not sexy, but it is important.

• COPYRIGHT
You can file copyright paperwork for your script and your final film. To file, go to the United States Library of Congress Copyright Office web site at *http://lcweb.loc.gov/copyright.*

• INSURANCE
Because you can't get it for free, ideally you'd like to avoid insurance. However, when it comes to securing the many things you want to get for free (such as equipment or locations), the owners won't give them to you unless you have the proper insurance. Additionally, SAG won't let you use their actors unless you have workers' comp. So unless you're using your own equipment and locations, hiring non-SAG performers, and are confident you won't be sued by someone, you probably will need to secure some sort of insurance policy. One of the best places to begin your insurance hunt is the SAG web site (*www.sag.org*), which has a section listing insurance brokers. Be careful about getting too large of a deductible because things do get broken, lost, or stolen. One filmmaker I know came back to set one morning to discover the dolly had been looted — and with it went the thousand dollars she had to pay for the deductible. As for workers' compensation insurance, even if you don't do it because SAG demands it, you might consider it just because people do get injured on set.

- *PERMISSION TO RECORD LIKENESS AGREEMENTS*

No one (except SAG!) is expecting you to do extensive paperwork for your short, but you do need some sort of agreement with your actors giving you permission to record their likeness. You don't want agreements so complicated that people feel like they have to consult with a lawyer before signing. A better choice than generating your own agreements is to buy preexisting generic permission forms — for talent, location, and even composer agreements — which can be ordered for a very reasonable price from Enterprise's web site (*www.enterpriseprinters.com*). If it's clear that you haven't generated the agreement (i.e., tampered with it to your advantage), most people are willing to sign without hesitation.

If you're doing behind-the-scenes on your short (and you really should — ask a friend with a mini-DV camera to go around and do a little "making of" — you might need it for the DVD), it's good to get everyone on the crew as well as the actors to sign a permission to record likeness release.

If you're shooting in a heavily populated area where real people are doing everyday business, put up signs warning the general public that there is filming going on and their likeness may be used in a short. For your protection, have your behind-the-scenes video camera document the sign so that you have proof a sign was posted.

- *LOCATION RELEASES*

Once again, a generic pre-existing form will do. Although Enterprise offers proper location releases, I've seen some people use the personal depiction release, scrawling "for house" and having the home owner sign and initial. However, if you're dealing with a more established entity like Jamba Juice or Ralph's grocery store, you'll want to present a more professional release.

- *TRADEMARK RELEASES*

Some studios are very careful about clearing everything, others figure as long as it's not used in a derogatory way they're safe using trademarked products as long as such products are not the main point of the scene. If it becomes a problem later on, you can always do the reality TV solution: blur out the trademark or logo in post.

On the other hand, you can emphasize the logos in exchange for product placement. Tell Coke you'll use only Coke products in the restaurant scene if they give you free drinks. Unfortunately, most companies know that shorts aren't seen by the general public so they'd rather save their placement for features. But you can always try.

PRODUCTION PAPERWORK IS EVEN SEXIER

There are computer programs that will generate breakdown sheets, shooting schedules, call sheets, production reports, etc., or you can buy blank generic forms from Enterprise. It's always good to do the work yourself, but if you can hire a line producer or a first assistant director to do production paperwork for you, do so! Paperwork can bog you down and sap all your creative energy. Leave it to the pros.

WHERE TO PUT ALL THIS WONDERFUL PAPER

Make a production book that you will have with you during preproduction, production, and post. Some people prefer the accordion style binder, others an old-fashioned three-ring notebook. It is your office in a box, and you'll find even years later you'll pull it out to refer to something. Paperwork is always important!

SECURING THE ESSENTIAL PEOPLE

How do you get people to work on your film — especially if you're not paying? The simple truth is everyone wants to be involved in good projects, and everyone likes to work with a talented filmmaker who is going to go far.

All you need is one crewmember to sign on and start the ball rolling. That crewmember will have worked enough productions that he or she can recommend others who might like to join

your show. The person to begin the process with is the person you will spend the most time with from start to finish: the producer. However, it's hard to get someone to produce your film because anyone who has produced a short knows how hard it is and is reluctant to do it again for no money. More than likely you'll be doing the producing yourself. Or you'll ask someone close to you who has no experience but is willing to share the workload with you.

The second best person to start with is your director of photography, who should be able to recommend people he or she has worked with in the past. How do you find a good DP? Watch short films made by filmmakers who live in your town. Note who shot them. Track down the filmmakers and ask if they would recommend their DP. While you're at it, ask for any other crew recommendation. Other methods: ask students in the local film school to shoot your project. Or ask the camera rental house to make recommendations. Asking rental houses is also a good way of finding other crewmembers. Soundmen can be found at sound rental houses, gaffers at lighting warehouses, etc.

ONE-MAN-BAND STYLE OF FILMMAKING
Like the director of *Bad Animals*, you might decide that you can borrow a mini-DV camera and shoot the short yourself. You might even forgo any additional crew, such as a soundperson or an art director. It's true, you can do everything yourself — but do you really want to?

PROS OF DOING EVERYTHING YOURSELF
- No workers' comp insurance necessary.

- No need to set aside money to feed the crew.

- You don't have to waste time communicating with other crewmembers.

- Without the distractions of others asking you production questions, you can put your full concentration on your actors.

- It's easier to get away with guerilla filmmaking if it's just you and a discreet camera rather than a full movie crew.

CONS OF DOING EVERYTHING YOURSELF

- It's a false reality. You're not learning how to deal with others, which is what you will be doing when you direct a bigger piece.

- No benefiting from the knowledge and experience of those who know more than you do.

- You're so busy doing everyone else's job (producing, lighting, arranging props) that you can't concentrate on doing your job: being a director.

- You can't do those other jobs as well as professionals can.

- You're overworking yourself when there's no reason to. Other people will be glad to crew your production for free if you ask them.

ASSEMBLING THE BARE MINIMUM CREW

Remember, the two things that kill most films are bad acting and bad sound. If you only have one other crew member, hire a sound mixer. You'll never regret having a good sound guy on set.

If you're going to layer in another crew member, and if your film is very visual, consider passing off the cinematography duties. Not only will a good director of photography know how to operate the camera better than you, he or she will light it more professionally than you ever could.

Lastly, if you can throw one other person into the mix, get someone to help you with production needs. This can be a producer, a coordinator, or a production assistant. It will make your job so much easier if there's someone to handle the myriad of things, big and small, that production entails.

STAFFING A "REAL" PRODUCTION

If "Everyone Works For Free!", why not expand into a properly staffed production company? If you're not paying anyone, it's tempting to keep on layering in the people. "I had fifty people on my flick," reports filmmaker Mat Fuller. "It was like a real movie for eight days." True, you're not paying them, but you do have to feed them, so it's not entirely a free ride. And if your crew gets too big, a lot of people sitting around chatting because they have nothing to do will kill your momentum. Better to have a lean, mean, fighting machine. Of course, if it's too lean with not enough hands to do things quickly, that's a problem. You'll find the correct balance for your project. Here's the twenty-six person crew (not including the director) I used when doing two-day productions with a 35mm camera:

PRODUCTION STAFF:

• *PRODUCER/UPM (UNIT PRODUCTION MANAGER)*
It's nice to have someone handle all the production details for you.

• *1ST A.D. (ASSISTANT DIRECTOR)*
The assistant director runs the set, keeping everything and everyone moving along. You'll find the only way to make it through an ambitious shoot schedule is to have a good first, who can keep you and the crew cracking along.

• *2ND A.D.*
If you must economize, try to get away without having a second A.D.

• *SCRIPT SUPERVISOR*
Another job that you might be tempted to axe, but think carefully before you do. Not only is the script supervisor there to take script notes, she is the director's second pair of eyes. While the director is thinking "big picture," the script supervisor is trained to keep an eye on details. She'll notice errors in continuity, crossing the line, etc. You'll regret it in post if you cut this crucial safety net.

• *P.A. (PRODUCTION ASSISTANT) X 3*
These are the hard workers who will be assigned to do anything and everything, on set and off. Because you'll always need an extra set of hands, legs or wheels, hire as many P.A.s as you can.

SET OPERATIONS:

• *KEY GRIP*
Grips are the ones who move the equipment and do the work that doesn't involve lighting (that's the gaffer's department). I always try to hire a key grip who comes with his own grip truck.

- *GRIP*

Usually, you need more than just a key grip.

- *DOLLY GRIP*

If you have a dolly, you need someone to push it. A good dolly grip does it effortlessly and smoothly, while a bad one will render your dolly shots useless.

SET DRESSING & PROPERTY:

- *ART DIRECTOR*

Many of our Fox Movie Channel shorts were shot on street corners where the real world was our art department. However, every production benefits from having a designated person making the location look good for camera. If you don't have a lot of money to spend, a good art director can whip up miracles you never would have expected on your limited budget. And production value does count for a lot in a short film.

- *PROPS PERSON*

A heavily art-directed short will require more than just one person in the art department. If you have many locations in your short, a props person will be assigned to keep everything straight on the hot set while the art director is off prepping or tearing down another set.

- *LEAD MAN*

Works with the art director to get things ready ahead of time.

- *P.A. (ART DEPT)*

A designated art department production assistant will move things along considerably.

WARDROBE:

- *COSTUME DESIGNER*

Quite often, the person in charge of wardrobe requires assistance. If your costumer asks to bring along their own assistant, agree only if this will help move things along. You don't want to be stingy, but every additional person is another mouth to feed. Perhaps the art department P.A. can help out.

CAMERA:

- *DP (DIRECTOR OF PHOTOGRAPHY)*

It's standard operating procedure on shorts for the DP to also function as the camera operator.

- *A.C. (ASSISTANT CAMERAPERSON)*

With film shoots, it's all about servicing the camera. The DP mostly likely has a team of A.C.s he or she likes to work with.

- *2ND A.C.*

If it makes the camera department work better and faster, let them have as many people as they need. Also, be prepared to be hit up for expendables from the camera department.

- *LOADER*

If you are using recanned film or short ends, you'd be wise to have someone dedicated to loading the camera magazines.

PRODUCTION SOUND:

- *SOUND ENGINEER*

Do not forget that the engineer is the second most important person on set. Make sure you pay attention when he or she suggests you to do certain things for sound. Most sound engineers come with their own equipment, which they request you rent from them. Even if they donate the equipment (good luck), they'll charge you for the DAT tapes and batteries used.

- *BOOM*

Usually the sound engineer has someone he or she is used to working with. If not, a P.A. can be recruited to handle the boom microphone, but be prepared for a lot of mistakes and inconsistencies.

LOCATION:

- *LOCATION MANAGER*

If you have a lot of locations, having someone scout, make deals, and be the liaison can be a wonderful thing.

MAKEUP & HAIRDRESSING:

- *MAKEUP & HAIR ARTIST*

Have one person do both, unless it's a very makeup-oriented project or there's a big female cast. If your film requires a lot of makeup or hair, pile on the artists to keep things on schedule in the morning, then release them before lunch so you don't have to feed them. Because they are using up their own supplies, your hair and makeup people will probably ask you for a kit fee.

LIGHTING:

- *GAFFER*

A well-lit film is worth its weight in gold. A DP can often act as his or her own gaffer, but everything will take longer (tweaking the lights always seems to take forever anyway!).

- *ELECTRICIAN*

Runs the power for the lights.

- *SWING*

Does both gaffing and gripping.

TOTAL CREW: 26

SHORT RECAP

- Ignore doing proper paperwork at your own peril.

- At the very least, get your actors to sign releases.

- You can buy generic production forms and legal agreements at a Hollywood store that specializes in this kind of paperwork: Enterprise of Hollywood, Printers and Stationers, *www.enterpriseprinters.com*.

- Assemble your crew by recommendations. Ask your DP to help you.

- Don't let your crew size get too big or you'll find yourself feeding an army!

CHAPTER 11

READY, STEADY, GO!

Finally, you're directing!

Every director will tell you that you can't spend enough time in preproduction. "I see a lot of people going into short filmmaking on a 'let's make a film! whim," remarks Brian McDonald, who wrote and directed the mocumentary *White Face*. "They get a lot of friends together, and it's 'let's put on a show!' That's not what I did. I approached my short no differently than I did the feature project I'm doing. I made sure the script was solid. I made sure I had really good actors. They

were auditioned, and they were good. I worked for years on my directing skills — still do." But sooner or later you're going to have to put on that baseball cap and say "action" and "cut."

TEN COMMON PRODUCTION PITFALLS TO AVOID

Although every production is unique, every filmmaker comes away with a "I'll never do that again" moment. Learn from our mistakes!

1

NOT PREPARED.

"The most important thing — and it's not redundant, it's not beating a cliché — you have to be prepared," warns *Coven* director Mark Borchardt. "I mean, there's no way around it. The more prepared you are, the more focused you are, the better results you'll see on screen. That goes for anyone, but it goes massively for people without any money. Because you can be a drunken lout if you got a hundred million dollars, the crew's going to do all the work for you; you're just going to incoherently point, and they'll bring you a masterpiece. Filmmakers without any money have to live off their means, their intelligence, their drive, their ambition. Because if they don't have a sterling professional crew, they have to fight to invent that quality in order to get it up on screen. And if you're slacking, man, if you don't get a proper microphone or stuff like that, it's going to show, it's going to damage you. Whatever or whoever you are as an independent filmmaker is going to show up on screen."

2

OBSESSING ABOUT THE WRONG THINGS.

Bad Animals filmmaker David Birdsell warns against "getting off track and getting overwhelmed by things that don't really matter, that aren't going to end up on screen. Usually there are so many logistics to deal with during production. The danger is that you spend all your time and energy fixing little things or moving a prop in the background, and forget that the whole focus of the scene should be on an important look on a character's face or the way a line is directed. When people watch the short later, they'll say, 'Did you see how bad that actor was?' No one will say, 'But the props were excellent.' So look out for logistics getting in the way of right priorities."

3

TOO AMBITIOUS FOR YOUR MONEY.

Don't try to stretch your production beyond what you can realistically accomplish. I know a directing team who jokingly referred to their extended and overly ambitious production and postproduction experience as "the *Apocalypse Now* of short filmmaking." Don't let this be you. If it's clear in preproduction that you're over your head and sinking fast, call a halt before you move into production. If you're already in production, scale back as you go. For example, extras — don't think you need fifty if can get away with thirty. Or locations. Rather than going from location to location, re-utilize the same location to avoid a series of moves.

4

CREW TOO FAT.

I was shocked when Mat Fuller told me he had fifty people on his crew. I thought my productions were fat with twenty-six. That's a lot of mouths to feed, and a lot of people just sitting around. Mat admits he had "about twenty too many, but in eight days we did one hundred and sixty shots, and a hundred and twenty set ups with a 35mm Panavision camera. That's a lot. Considering there wasn't one pro on the crew!"

5

CREW TOO UNSKILLED. OR TOO SKILLED.

Yes, shorts are a learning experience for everyone. But you don't want everyone to be at kindergarten level when you need high school seniors to make it through your day. "If you're not paying them, anything goes at any time," prompts Mark Borchardt, whose production woes were documented in *American Movie.* "I have some professional people that work with me recording sound, etc., who give up their time because they believe in the work. And then there's other people who are passed out in the kitchen by 11 am, you know, from drinking. It's quite a polar experience."

Conversely, be wary of pros used to big budget extravaganzas who can't go back to guerilla style filmmaking. Directors of photography who work extensively on high profile commercials are particularly worrisome. They'll want all their toys, and can even help you get them, but sometimes you won't want them. I've been on sets where precious time was wasted waiting for the crane operator to get ready, when there was no need for a crane in the first place.

6

ACTORS TOO USED TO FEATURE WORK.

On a similar note, actors who are used to doing many takes on big features don't understand that you have limited film stock. They also don't understand about the rough shooting conditions. The last thing you need is someone complaining about not having their own trailer.

7

SKIPPING CUTAWAY SHOTS.

It's easy when you're trying to make it through an ambitious shot list to try to skip over things you'll need later for editing. Like cutaway shots.

8.

SLOPPY SHOOTING.

Fans of *American Movie* send Mark Borchardt their own work to watch. "Half of the people haven't even heard of or understand what a tripod is,"

Borchardt laughs. "It's amazing and bizarre at the same time. You would have doubled, tripled your production value by simply putting the camera on a tripod. I don't understand that! Also they haven't studied enough film to understand how to shoot, and how that shooting is going accommodate the editing process. The shots don't match, the shots jump. They don't understand the 180 degree rule, they don't understand the 30% change rules. These are not rules for rules' sake. These are rules that give quality and flow and natural velocity to images on screen. You have to educate yourself. For example, the 180 degree rule is that when characters face each other and you're doing reverse shots back and forth, the camera has to stay on a chosen side of both of the actors so on the screen it looks like they're actually talking to each other. I've seen horrible Christian films where these guys are talking back and forth into outer space, it's bizarre!"

Filmmakers who don't pay attention to crossing the line also irritate *Beeker's Crossing* director Robbie Consing. "Motion has to be kept consistent," Consing points out. "So basically if the good guys are charging at the enemy left to right, and the enemy charges right to left, you have to keep it that way. Let's say you're depicting a football game in a movie. Yes, the camera will go handheld. Yes, you'll have shots from the stadium and the blimp. But if it's not made very clear that left to right means losing, and right to left means winning, you violated a simple part of film vocabulary."

Other mistakes include getting the actors' eye lines wrong, which becomes obvious in editing when the direction a character is looking doesn't match the reverse angle or a P.O.V. shot, or not framing the actor with enough head room (not enough space between the top of the frame and the top of the actor's head) or nose room (from the tip of the actor's nose to the edge of the frame).

8
SHOOTING TOO MUCH

For *I'm on Fire*, director Ryan Rowe had a ten-to-one shooting ratio. Because most scenes were locked down master shots (he had to do that for special effects reasons), Rowe decided to use his ten-to-one ratio by shooting each master shot ten times. When it came to editing, he couldn't decide which one of the ten was superior.

I've also seen filmmakers fall in the trap of "shooting one more for safety" early in the day, taking up so much time that by the end of the day, to get all their scheduled shots they had to do one take only and move on. So much for one more for safety!

9

NOT PAYING ENOUGH ATTENTION TO SOUND.

Listen to what your sound person says and wants. If they request room tone, stop and let them have room tone. Filmmaker Jordan Horowitz shares a sound disaster. "While making my one and ONLY digital short in Los Angeles, I had horrible sound problems," says Horowitz. "My sound guy was the only paid crew member, getting $200/day, and the only one who proved totally incompetent. Day 1: Boom microphone running directly into camera. Playback days recordings: no audio. Instead, loud Latin music over everything. Somehow, he had honed in on some radio station, and that's all we got. Re-shots needed.

"Day 2: Shooting on boat. Could not boom into camera. No DAT or Nagra. Sound guy recommended recording on MiniDisc. Record entire day of sync sound — sound guy ejects disc without finalizing; i.e., there's no table of contents on disc, making it unreadable by any computer or player. About six months later, we were somehow able to recover contents of disc, only to find the audio sounded like total garbage anyway. We wound up using the camera's microphone and filtering out all the hisses and hums.

"What sucked most about the sound guy was his attitude. He acted like he was too good for this 'ghetto production,' despite getting paid. After dropping him, I hired a guy who had never done sound before, but had a great attitude to learn. He recorded the rest of the shoot without a single hitch. By the way, that sound guy didn't mention the minidisc problem to me at all. He took his paycheck and split, and just before leaving whispered it to the gaffer, who was forced to be the one to inform me."

10

SAYING YOU'LL FIX IT IN POST, COUNTING ON RESHOOTS.

If you always think you can go back or fix it later, you'll get sloppy. It's cheaper to do things right the first time. If you're shooting on tape, review footage before wrapping a location. That's the beauty of tape — you don't have to wait for the film to come back from the lab to discover if anything is wrong. However, it's tempting to waste time viewing and reviewing what you've already shot. Operate under the assumption that things are fine, but do your "idiot check" before you move on and can't go back.

SHORT RECAP:

- Shorts are a learning experience for everyone.

- Assemble your crew wisely. Not too large. Not too inexperienced. Just right.

- Use a tripod!

- Don't plan on reshooting. Get what you need during production.

- Enjoy the process!

CHAPTER 12

POSTPRODUCTION FOR FILM AND TAPE

Get your film out of the can without going broke.

Let's be honest — postproduction is a hideously painful process. Every step takes longer and costs much more than you want it to. Things go wrong all the time, and everyone blames someone else for the problems. Worst of all, you're forced to face

the film you actually did shoot rather than the film you thought you shot. Fortunately, it all comes together in the end — when you see that you really do have a film you can be proud of. Then you'll forget about all the pain and suffering of post, just like you did with all the pain and suffering of pre-production and production. And you'll want to do it all over again.

The most important thing to remember about post is that, unlike production, you have no concrete time frame. You can take your time arranging for freebies. However, whenever you are paying (especially by the hour), you need to go as fast as possible.

HOW TO GET YOUR FILM FROM "IN THE CAN" INTO THE EDITING SYSTEM

If you shot film (as opposed to video), you need to find a lab to develop the negative and prep it for telecine. Because labs charge by the foot, if you have very little footage, you might be able to beg for free processing. Perhaps your DP has a lab that he or she has done a lot of jobs at and therefore can ask a favor or two. If you have to pay the lab, take consolation in the fact that developing and prepping the footage for telecine aren't your biggest expenses in post. Also, the future of your entire film rests on the continued well-being of your negative. Don't risk mishaps occurring at an inexpert lab. Better to beg a discount at a professional lab than risk an unmitigated disaster at a fly-by-night company.

Once the negative has been developed, in order to see your footage you need to do telecine. During this process, your negative is run through a machine, a color timer makes adjustments, then the image is laid down on tape. A good timer can perform miracles in telecine. If there is something that is terribly wrong with what you shot, mention it to the colorist and see what he or she can do.

However, be aware that such magic has only been done on your video footage. Your original negative is in the same shape it always was. If you want to go back to print, you'll be dismayed when you discover that those problems remain.

The telecine step is a prime example of how things in post can be done for free or can cost outrageous amounts. I've paid as much as $400 an hour for telecine, and I've also gotten free service (although tape is rarely free). That's why it's so hard to budget for post. Three hours of telecine could cost you $1,200 or $0 (plus tape).

If you have extremely limited telecine time, you might be forced to lay down only your preferred takes or skip syncing up sound at this stage and wait to marry sound with picture during editing. Don't allow yourself or your DP to get lost in the magic of telecine. As you know from shooting, some DPs will tweak forever. If you're paying by the hour, you need to keep the work-flow going. Sometimes to get the best deal, you have to agree to unsupervised telecine. Meaning you and your DP can't be there. If this is your only option, take it.

If you do get free or severely discounted telecine time, you'll probably be working late at night and on bumpable hours (meaning if a paying client comes, you're bumped) and with the less experienced color timers. If you're never planning on going back to your original negative, it's worth paying for a good color timer who can work fast and give you the best results. After all, this is the stage where your film's look is solidifying. Why suffer with five free hours with a lame colorist when one paid hour with a kick ass miracle worker is worth its weight in gold? Another option is to do unsupervised telecine for your raw footage, and then book time to color correct after editing when you have a locked picture.

Be aware that you can beg free telecine, but quite often the tape stock isn't free. Think of tape stock as the "expendables" of post. If you lay your footage down to DigiBeta, it can get very pricey fast. Speaking of tape stock, you should have already chosen your editor (even it's just you) so you'll know what format you'll need for editing.

FROM "IN THE CAN" TO "IN THE EDITING SYSTEM": TAPE

How easy is this? If you shoot on tape, you don't even have to take the stock out of the camera! Just wire your camera up to the computer and begin to edit.

TIME OUT FOR EDITING

Before you begin editing, know your footage. This is definitely a "free" step that you should spend a lot of time on. It's time to make a log of all your footage. Note the time code, the scene and take number, what works, and what doesn't. This is you putting the film together in your head. During this process, refer to your storyboards, script supervisor notes, and any notes you might have scribbled down during telecine. You might even go as far as making a paper edit — listing the takes in the order you'd assemble them if you were doing a linear edit. Not only does this help you become familiar with the film you actually did shoot, it will save you invaluable time in editing.

With the proliferation of desktop editing systems such Adobe Premiere or Apple's Final Cut Pro, you really can edit your film yourself on your home computer. But just because you can do something doesn't mean you should. Many short filmmakers edit their own work. This is the reason why too many shorts are too long. You don't have the distance to be objective. "A lot of people opt to edit their own movie," points out filmmaker Amy Talkington. "On one level, that's great, you learned a lot about editing. On the other hand, it's very valuable to learn how to work with an editor. When you make a feature, you're going to have an editor." A good editor is like a good DP — they'll make everything look better than you ever could doing it yourself.

TEN COMMON EDITING PITFALLS

1

FEATURE FILM PACING.

I'll say it again: you are not making a feature!

2

STARTING A SCENE TOO EARLY, ENDING IT TOO LATE.

Remember back when you were writing your script you tried to start each scene as late as possible and end it as soon as possible? The same thing applies in editing. If you start a scene with a character walking somewhere, know that one day Noah Edelson is going to see your short and yell at the character, "It's a short film — you should be there already!"

3

FALLING IN LOVE WITH YOUR TEMP MUSIC.

It's perfectly acceptable to use pre-recorded music as a temp track during editing. Problems arise when you get so attached to that Stones song that you can't imagine any other kind of music ever being as good. We'll cover music in more detail in the next chapter.

4

SUFFERING FROM TIRED EYES.

Even if you're working with an editor, you're too close to your material to be the final arbiter. Throughout the editing process, bring in people who aren't familiar with your film to give you a fresh perspective.

5

NOT LISTENING TO HONEST CRITIQUES.

"What I've noticed is most filmmakers want advice," remarks director/editor Tara Veneruso, "but when they get it, they're like, 'Oh, but you don't understand why we did it like this.' They're not actually open to listening. So many people get into that over-defensive mode, which is a mistake. Usually, somebody will only give you advice if they actually want to help you!"

Festival programmer Jennifer Stark points out that critiques aren't limited to the editing room. "You can get so caught up in having made a film that you lose sight that you've made a film," remarks Stark. "You feel that you've created something so unique, so special. And you surround yourself with your friends, who want to be helpful so they'll say great and wonderful things. Then you'll put yourself in an environment like a festival, and you might hear for the first time something that's not as positive about your film, but very constructive. I think you do need to listen. Because I think people in the festivals are very passionate about films. All they want is for films to be better."

6

HAVING A TITLE SEQUENCE.

Features have time for a fancy title or opening credits sequence. Shorts don't. Every filmmaker who loads the front of his or her film with credits regrets it. Don't do it. However, it isn't a bad idea to make a quick logo that plays in front of your film. The reason being, a short film is usually the first thing projected in a festival situation, and if the projectionist is a little slow in doing everything right, the very first few seconds of your film can get cut off, or have too loud sound, or no sound. A very quick logo can be your sacrificial victim. With the Fox Movie Channel shorts, our logo was eight seconds long — and that was much too long.

7

TOO LONG END CREDIT SEQUENCE.

Credits are free on video, but not on film. Any typed words that you generate in editing don't exist on film so you will have to either beg or pay to have them made if you plan on striking a film print. If you feel like you must thank anyone and everyone who had anything to do with your film in the credits, consider doing an alternate video version of your film that has the never-ending credits roll. For the "real world" (festivals and potential television sales), keep your end credits to a reasonable length.

8

NOT INCLUDING A WEB SITE IN YOUR CREDITS.

Put your film's web site at the very end of the credits and leave it up long enough for people to remember it. That way anyone watching your film can contact you. More about your film's web site in Chapter 15.

9

INCORRECT COPYRIGHT NOTICE.

Don't forget your copyright notice at the end of the film: "© 2004 Jane Filmmaker". If your film is finished at the tail end of one year, chose the following year as your copyright.

10

EDL NOT CONFIGURED FOR NEGATIVE CUTTER.

If you're going back to film, make sure your editing system can generate an EDL (edit decision list) that a film negative cutter can use. Have your editor consult with the negative cutter if you're not sure.

MOVING ON TO SOUND

It doesn't matter how pretty your film looks — if the sound is sucky, people will think your film is sucky. Spend the time to do this right. Great sound will add so much more production value. For one of our Fox Movie Channel shorts, we got to spend a day with the Disney foley artists. Wow! I can't tell you how impressive that short's sound is! In fact, I don't think I'll ever want to go back to lesser-quality sound houses. I know another short filmmaker who got free sound work at Lucas's Skywalker facility (he had connections). Use your short film mantras ("one day you'll be a paying client," "it's less time commitment than a feature") to see what you can beg for free. Don't be afraid to aim high.

When you're doing your final sound sessions, if you possibly can swing it, try to create a Music and Effects track (commonly known as an M&E track). Having a dialogue-free track is important for foreign television sales, where certain stations won't take your film unless they can dub it into their own language. If your film has no dialogue to begin with, you've got a de facto M&E track, and this is a non-issue for you. However, most short filmmakers who are doing professional sound mixes on a dialogue-heavy film can't beg enough post time to create an M&E track. If you can't, resign yourself to licensing your film to networks that will do subtitles.

As for your final sound format, some short filmmakers have gotten very fancy with digital soundtracks that are so high end that the projectors used at most regional film festivals can't handle it. Settle for Dolby SR; it works everywhere and is more than adequate for a short.

BEHOLD YOUR FINAL VIDEO MASTER

Your video master should be on the best format you can achieve. In some cases, it might be a mini-DV tape or a DVD. If you can swing it, DigiBeta is your best master format. For the Fox Movie Channel shorts, we mastered to the D2 format because that was the best format our sound house could handle (no DigiBeta deck). Imagine my horror when I moved into DVD production and heard that D2 is a terrible master format for DVD. Avoid D2!

You can have a "letterboxed" master, but also make sure you have a full screen version for television and internet sales (many networks won't take anything but full screen).

Your master should begin with sixty seconds of bars and tone, followed by thirty seconds of black. When you make VHS screening dubs, leave off the bars and tone, and have five seconds of black at most. Your picture should start at even time code hour. Nondrop frame time code is preferred.

Your audio should be:

Channel 1: stereo mix

Channel 2: stereo mix

Channel 3: dialogue (if at all possible)

Channel 4: music and effects (if at all possible)

ONE LAST WORD ABOUT PAPERWORK

In addition to the EDL (edit decision list) which you will give to the negative cutter if you go back to film, there are two other major lists you need to collect during this phase of post.

- *DIALOGUE LIST*

This is a basic time-code referenced listing of every piece of dialogue in your film. You'll need to provide this list to foreign festivals and foreign television stations if they are going to translate your film.

- *MUSIC CUE SHEET*

This is a time-code referenced listing of every piece of music in your film. You'll need to provide this list to television stations who will pay royalties. We'll go over the music cue sheet in more detail in the following chapter.

DON'T FORGET TO FILE A COPYRIGHT ON THE FINISHED FILM

Visit the Library of Congress Copyright Office web site (*http://lcweb.loc.gov/copyright*) for specifics.

FINISHING ON FILM

Because very few shorts have any hope of theatrical exhibition, the only reason you need a film print is to screen at festivals. "If they can afford it, most filmmakers want a film print," sighs short film distributor Carol Crowe of Apollo Cinema. "For them, it's like a romance. The best thing in the world is to sit in a dark room, see the flicker and hear the sound of the projector. And most of the film festivals right now — in a couple of years, it will totally change — but right now, most of the festivals prefer film. In the future, it will be more digital projection. The thing filmmakers need to be open to, and a lot of them aren't right now because they're in love with film and very stubborn, is digitizing their shorts to be projected digitally. Think about how much you're going to save on print trafficking and wear and tear!"

MAKING A FILM PRINT

If you're going back to film, there are quite a few more steps after you've completed your video master.

- *TITLES CREATED – THEN SENT TO NEGATIVE CUTTER TO BE CUT INTO THE FILM.*

Anything that isn't on the original negative has to be created if you're going back to film. So your credits that you created on the editing system need to be created on film — and it's very expensive if you don't get it for free. A better option is to figure out a way to shoot your own titles and credits. I've seen film titles and credits written in sand on the beach, embroidered on clothes hanging on a clothes line, arranged with magnetic letters on a refrigerator door, and even done up with ransom note-style clippings.

- *OPTICALS CREATED — THEN SENT TO NEGATIVE CUTTER TO BE CUT INTO THE FILM.*

Any digital wizardry you did in editing that doesn't exist on the negative also has to be shot on film — it's called an optical. Those slow motion shots you did in the computer? An optical. The split screen? An optical.

- *COMPUTER-GENERATED SPECIAL EFFECTS OUTPUT TO NEGATIVE — THEN SENT TO NEGATIVE CUTTER TO BE CUT INTO THE FILM.*

All those "free" special effects you generated in the computer? No longer so free when you want to output them to film. For the Fox Movie Channel short *I'm on Fire*, we did the fire digitally. Then we went to a high end special effects house that outputs to film negative — and charges per frame. Yes, per frame. As in 24fps. We ended up paying thousands of dollars for our "free" fire.

- *OPTICAL SOUNDTRACK CREATED FROM YOUR FINAL SOUND MIX. THE OPTICAL TRACK AND THE CUT NEGATIVE CAN BE MARRIED AT THE NEGATIVE CUTTER OR AT THE LAB.*

Remember your sound doesn't exist on film yet. You need to have an optical track created. This is another step worth trying to beg for free but ultimately isn't that expensive if you have pay for it. I never had any trouble with sound not syncing, but other filmmakers have. If you're begging, it's harder to get your problems fixed in a timely manner.

- *THE NEGATIVE CUTTER GOES TO WORK.*

The negative cutter assembles negative and attaches an Academy leader to the front of your film. You can try to beg for free negative cutting, which usually is billed per ten-minute reel with a maximum amount of cuts. But do you want some trainee potentially ruining your irreplaceable negative when negative cutting isn't that expensive for one-reel films? If your short is five minutes long, try to pay half rate. For *I'm On Fire*, we did beg free negative cutting since we already had the bulk of the film assembled when we did that super-expensive special effects output. All the negative cutter had to do was splice the opening and closing credits on.

- *COLOR TIMING OF PRINT*

The cut negative and optical track are sent to your lab to strike a film print. Now comes the fun part — seeing your film projected for the very first time on the big screen. Similar to the telecine step, once again there's a color timer who makes adjustments. Unlike the digital wizardry of telecine, there are only so many adjustments your timer can make with film processing.

While it's easy to get obsessed with unfixable details as you finish the last step in creating your film, it's important to stop and appreciate the fact that your film is now being projected on the big screen. Your little idea is now a movie. This is a very big deal!

- *WALK OUT THE DOOR WITH AN ANSWER PRINT.*
  ORDER MORE RELEASE PRINTS AS NEEDED.

Sometimes you walk away with the final answer print and never order more release prints. If you become successful on the festival circuit, you'll need more than one print. For some of our most popular Fox Movie Channel shorts, we had eleven prints in circulation all over the world.

A QUICKER WAY TO GO FROM VIDEO MASTER TO FILM PRINT

While all the previous postproduction steps take forever, involve dealing with many different vendors and result in problem after problem, the tape-to-film transfer process is all handled by one vendor, and you personally don't have to arrange for any of it. You give the company your video master, and approximately four days later you come back to see your film print. How fast and easy is that?!

Generally, these companies charge by the running time of your film. If your piece is very short, paying by the minute isn't so bad. Here's the bad news: Tape-to-film prints don't look nearly as good as a cut-film-negative-to-film prints. As soon as you see your tape-to-film print projected after a properly done print, you realize how much you compromised. However, at most festivals, your film is not projected in the most pristine circumstances. Consequently, everyone's film looks about as bad as yours! It's also important to remember that many festivals can screen your work on video nowadays. There's no stigma attached to not having a print. "We show films that were shot on video, then transferred to film," says Sundance Film Festival senior programmer Trevor Groth. "We also show films shot on video and projected on video. We also have shown work shot on film but then transferred to HD, and projected on video. Whatever works best for the filmmaker, whatever makes the most sense aesthetically and financially, we accommodate." Rather than investing time and money in getting a film print, you might better invest that money in getting a great video master.

INSIDER INFORMATION ABOUT DVD

It's more than likely that DVD is going to be the final format your film lives on. "VHS is dead as far as I'm concerned," swears filmmaker Roy Unger. "I have a box of ninety copies of my short, *Requiem*, that I'll probably never show to anybody. The DVDs I can burn on my Macintosh are so much better quality. Better sound, and they don't drop out. You can package them so they look like a real DVD. If I put mine on the video shelf, I defy a regular consumer to know that mine's not done by a studio!"

Jess Bowers, who has authored the *Band Of Brothers* and *The Sopranos* box sets for HBO and the *Fellowship of the Rings Special Edition* for New Line, has also authored many short film collections. He strongly recommends that short filmmakers embrace DVD technology and do it themselves. "Burners are relatively inexpensive nowadays," Bowers swears. "If you want to make a DVD for your personal use, if you don't want a lot of control over the presentation of the material, use whatever software comes with the burner. But if you want a really dynamic interface, you're looking at purchasing something like Adobe's Encore product, Apple's DVD Studio Pro, or Sonic Solutions' authoring packages for the PC. For about $500, you can get yourself the DVD authoring equivalent of Photoshop.

"If you're creating a lot of DVDs — for instance, you're going to sell your short in stores — you have two ways of going. You can burn a bunch of

DVD-Rs at home. Or for small scale duplication, it really pays to go with what's called a replicator. A replicator would make a whole bunch of copies for you, print some nice cover artwork, and then put it in a case. A thousand discs might cost you somewhere in the neighborhood of a couple grand, but you're going to save yourself a lot of trouble. And you're going to end up with a disc that's going to be playable in 100% of DVD players (which is not always the case with DVD-Rs)."

Asked what format you master your film on if you're planning on making DVDs, Jess explains that "MPEG2 (MPEG is the video format that DVD uses) is a component digital format. So you want to avoid any kind of composite video format. VHS is out. 3/4 is out. D2 is out. You'll want to stick with component video formats. And digital is best. So D1, or a Digital Betacam, or a D5 are going to be your best bet. Short of that, you'll have a lot of people with analog component formats — like BetacamSP. For the most part, the simple answer is DigiBeta is probably the best most versatile format for DVD mastering, and then the other subformats would be BetacamSP, or mini-DV.

"I know a lot of short filmmakers are working in mini-DV, which is a great format. It is, in fact, a component digital format, although not the best component digital format because it's also compressed. And it also doesn't have a perfect color space. But if you've kept it completely in the DV format the whole way — if you shot on DV, then you edited on DV — go ahead and keep it on DV to go to DVD. If you're working in Final Cut Pro, which is a very popular editor right now, you have the option of saving that out as a Quicktime file. One of the other options is saving it out as an MPEG2 file. So you can go directly from your Final Cut Pro sequence (and on the PC side you've got things like Avid and Premiere — they also have very similar options). Basically, you can go straight out of your Final Cut Pro sequence to MPEG2 files. That's also an option, and a pretty good option, in fact. Maybe not as high a quality as some of these higher end MPEG2 hardware encoders like we would use, obviously, but it's a pretty good option."

Jess' last words of advice: "One of the things that's really important for short films (and really any DVD project) is good graphic design. You want to make sure you get somebody — if you can't do it yourself, find a friend or a service bureau of some sort — that can design both the packaging and the on-screen menus for you. Because it's all about the presentation with

DVD. You've got a little canvas there, and you can really make it look slick. Or you can keep it simple. If you want to get noticed and make your stuff look really great, have good menu and package design."

SHORT RECAP

- Post can be time-consuming and frustrating.

- Know from the start if you're going back to film. Your end product affects many stages in the post process.

- Just because you think you can edit your film yourself doesn't mean you should.

- If you do want to go back to film and your piece isn't very long, tape-to-film transfer is a viable option.

- If you burn your own DVDs, there might be a compatibility issue with older DVD players not able to play them. However, most newer players have no problem with DVD-Rs.

CHAPTER 13

WHY MUSIC WILL
KILL YOU

*W**hen it comes to making the soundtrack of your dreams a reality, you might have to make a few artistic and financial compromises.*

The simplest thing to do is to hire a composer to make an original score. Buy a blank composer agreement from Enterprise Printers. Have your composer

sign it. Your composer creates a killer score from scratch and turns in a music cue sheet — and you're done. Easy. No outstanding licensing fees. You're free and clear to sell your film anywhere.

Unfortunately, most filmmakers want to include already existing music, to have a hit-filled soundtrack like feature films have. It's true, "real music" adds so much more production value to your film. Many of my favorite short films incorporate already existing songs. And that's why you'll never see them — the filmmakers couldn't afford the music rights for commercial exhibition. "You've got to have your music clearances," emphasizes Megan O'Neill of AtomShockwave. "And that doesn't mean just for festivals. If you want your film to be sold — and I've never met a filmmaker who afterwards didn't want their film to be sold — do not use music you haven't paid for. If it's too late and you've already got festival-only rights, then change the music. Maybe not necessarily in your festival prints, but certainly in everything else."

Film sales agent and distributor David Russell of Big Film Shorts stresses the importance of not tying up your film's future with bad choices during postproduction. "The thing I wish I could get across to filmmakers," Russell says, "especially if you haven't made your film yet, is ask yourself truly and honestly why you are making the film. If it's just to have a calling card so you can get a meeting with a studio executive or an agent (or try to, anyway!), then use music you don't own. It's not legal, but you aren't going to get busted for it. Put anybody on the soundtrack if you think it's going to goose up the watchability of your film. Go ahead and put the Rolling Stones on the soundtrack. They're only a million dollars a song, no matter how you use it. But if you think at any point you'll want to make a dollar on your film (and I think all filmmakers do nowadays), you have to make the film legal."

Director David Birdsell was put in a situation where he had festival rights for two crucial songs in his student film, *Blue City*, but he couldn't license his short to television because he couldn't afford the rights to those two crucial songs. He ended up substituting two alternate songs for television. Nobody who hadn't seen the original would ever realize the televised version didn't showcase the director's first choice in music. But the filmmaker knows that version is the "compromised" version of his film. "Music can be one of the most important things in a film," says Birdsell, "so don't run away from it because you think there will be a problem. Everything in making a film is a problem. If there's something that is really going to help your film, do your best to get it. Music is important. All things being equal, it will make your life easier if you can wrap up the music rights beforehand."

Mark Osborne's short, *More*, is set to an entire New Order song. Did he secure the music in advance? "I got the permission after I made the film," Osborne admits. "I got permission from the band, but I didn't know until way late in the game that I needed permission from the label. It was a big pain."

Whether you do the legwork in advance or late in the game, securing music rights will be a big pain.

HOW TO GET A FRANK SINATRA SONG

In fact, it is annoying but fairly easy to score free (or very cheap) festival licenses for pretty major songs. Just like your dealings with SAG, the people who administer music licenses will treat you professionally if you deal with them professionally. If you have your heart set on including Frank Sinatra singing "My Way" in your film, here's how you do it.

First, you have to realize that you're actually asking for two licenses. One is the right to use the song, the other the performance. For example, the song "My Way" has been recorded by many acts including Sid Vicious, Elvis Presley, and Frank Sinatra. You need to secure the rights for the song itself (the sync license). Then you have to get permission to use the Frank Sinatra recording of it (the master license). If you want one of your characters to sing the song himself in your film (rather than using the already recorded Sinatra version), all you need is the sync license. But for Sinatra's version, you need both.

To find out who controls the sync rights, look on the CD — the publishing company is usually listed right under the song title. As for who controls the master rights, it's usually the record label itself.

So you're approaching two different organizations. The way it usually works is you can get the master rights for the same amount you're paying for the sync rights. Start with the sync rights since there's no point in getting the label to say yes if you can't get permission to use the song.

There are two terms you need to master before you begin this adventure:

- *GRATIS*
A fancy way of saying our favorite word: "Free."

- *MOST FAVORED NATION*
Which means no one will be paid more than this company. In other words, if the publishing company agrees to a $500 most favored nation license fee, and the record label holds firm at $750 for the master rights, you have to go back to the publishing company and give them another $250 to equal what you agreed to pay the record company.

INSIDER INFORMATION ON GETTING WEEZER SONGS

Filmmaker Karl Hirsch made a short called *Media Whore*, which featured Weezer's hit "Hash Pipe." "Our short is essentially a series of interview clips with an idiot VJ," Hirsch explains. "We wanted to cut it together as hip, cool, and MTV-like as possible. In editing, we used temp music — the latest, hippest, coolest music from Fat Boy Slim, Weezer, and everybody you can think of. When we were all done, we knew we had to replace all the temp music with music we could realistically afford the rights to. What we did for most of the music is call a couple of composers and ask them to take a song and copycat it so it sounds close but it isn't really the original song, it's actually a brand new song. However, one of our songs was crucial, a song by Weezer, and we wanted to get temporary festival rights for it. I ended up finding the publisher, sent him the movie. It took him forever, but he came back and approved it. Universal approved it. We paid $2 for a one-year festival run only. $1 each for sync and master use. Not bad considering 'Hash Pipe' is Weezer's biggest hit song! The paper on which the sync and master use agreements were printed on was probably worth more than a dollar each! One thing that I found out is a lot of artists are retaining their own publishing. So when I found the publisher, it was essentially a publishing agent which handles people like me for people like Rivers Cuomo, who as the songwriter owns Weezer's songs. So all I had to do is call this guy, and he called up Rivers and said, 'You want to do it?' It was that easy. It probably took about five weeks. My experience is you usually have to go to the publisher first, and the record company will match whatever the publisher says."

IT'S EASY TO FAX A LICENSE REQUEST

When you're approaching publishers and record labels to request a music license, it's important to be professional. Mara Schwartz, who licensed music for the DVD series *Circuit*, suggests you prepare a memo with the following information:

- *YOUR CONTACT INFORMATION*

Your name, relationship to the film (producer, director, etc.), and contact information, including your address, fax number, and e-mail address.

- *DESCRIPTION OF YOUR FILM PROJECT*

Including the title, story synopsis, and the fact that it is a short film.

- *INFO ON THE SONG*

The title of the song you are requesting permission to use. The songwriter/publisher. (You get this information from the CD.) The record label.

TYPE OF USE REQUESTED

How exactly the song is used in the context of the scene (e.g., in the foreground or background, under the credits, etc.)

LENGTH OF USE REQUESTED

How many seconds of the song you are asking to use.

TERRITORY REQUESTED

If you don't want restrictions on where the film can be shown, request "worldwide."

RIGHTS REQUESTED

Festival only or television, Internet, DVD, etc.

TERM LENGTH REQUESTED

If you don't want to limit the length of time your film can be shown, request "in perpetuity."

LICENSE FEE REQUESTED

Your obvious first choice: gratis.

Mara Schwartz adds, "This seems like a lot to think about, but all this information needs to be put in writing to avoid problems later. You can always hire a music clearance company or music supervisor to do this legwork for you, but somebody needs to make sure music is cleared properly or there will be headaches and hold-ups down the line."

INSTEAD, HIRE A COMPOSER

"Here's my big advice: use original music," counsels *Breezeway* director George Langworthy. "The world is filled with amazingly talented musicians. They're right around the corner, they're cool, and they're dying to do great work. If you say you need a film score, even people who are very successful musicians will do it. I've had amazing luck with very big bands."

As with every step in the filmmaking process, you need to choose your people wisely. *Life After Death* filmmaker Jordan Horowitz had a telling experience. "I knew my last film would be heavily music driven, and therefore hired a composer at the very beginning of postproduction," recounts Horowitz. "I wasn't impressed by his reel but thought he had a good attitude and would be easy to communicate with. Eight months later, on the day he was to deliver a music cut, I discovered how wrong I had read him. He was completely condescending, and told me this is his cut, and if any changes whatsoever were needed, I would need to hire someone else. With that said, I prayed he had composed something at least decent. It was total crap. Looked as if he hadn't even watched the film for which he was composing. So I left the music with him, and walked out. It did work out for the best as later I found an inexperienced but talented kid with the right attitude who composed a terrific score."

Don't be afraid to approach anyone. "I knew I wanted to have this sort of goofy, charming story song at the end of my film," says *Second Skin* director Amy Talkington, who is fearless about tracking down people. "And something I thought of was *Welcome to the Dollhouse*, the music in that movie. So I looked at that movie's credits, I saw the woman's name. Called information. She was listed. Called her up. She loved my movie and wrote a song. She also did the music for another short of mine that had a goofy song. She did them both for a tiny deferred fee."

DON'T FORGET ABOUT THE MUSIC CUE SHEET

Whether you use pre-existing songs or new material composed specifically for your short, you'll need to keep a record of how much music was used in the film and where it was used. "A music cue sheet," explains film sales agent Carol Crowe, "has the title of the song, the cue in the movie where it comes in, the name of the composer or publisher, and who to pay music royalties into (BMI or ASCAP). If your composer isn't a member of BMI or ASCAP, he or she should join. Or you can write on the music cue sheet that no royalties are owed anywhere because no one is affiliated with any societies." This information is given to television channels that license your film for broadcast and therefore must pay music royalties. "Most filmmakers think this is going to cost them money," remarks Crowe. "It doesn't cost the filmmaker. It's the TV station that pays. For the composer, if it turns out to be a hot short film, I'm sure over time it can actually add up!"

SHORT RECAP

- To license already recorded songs, you need to secure both a sync license and a master license.

- You can get major recording artists to give you reasonable licensing fees if you ask for festival only rights.

- However, it's nearly impossible to get those rights for any kind of commercial sales.

- Consider having an artistically compromised version of your film for television sales.

- Music cue sheets are necessary for royalty payments.

PART III:

MARKETING YOUR FILM

CHAPTER 14

CREATING A GAME PLAN

Time to launch your film and yourself.

Now what? Now comes the marketing and distribution plan for not only your film, but for yourself and your future career. It can be overwhelming, but remember you didn't sacrifice all that blood, sweat, money, time, and tears for nothing. The whole point was to make something you wanted to show to other people.

"The term I came up with after doing all this press and promotion was 'prestitute' - that's what I felt like," jokes filmmaker Roy Unger. "But the reason I made my film, *Requiem*, was as a calling card. So the concept of the film was to promote me as a director, not just the film. And it goes hand in hand. I mean, I am my film. If important people like the film, they might hire me to make another one, which is the whole point. When you market yourself, you need to get yourself out there. Nobody else is going to do it. You're basically a press agent. I didn't fully understand what a press agent does until I became my own."

Short film programmer Joel S. Bachar adds, "What I see is that people end up with a short film, and they don't know what to do with it. Of course, everybody wants to get into Sundance, and you know most people don't. Make up a target list of festivals, and think of the costs of submitting not only entry fees, but all the ancillary materials that go with it. People don't realize it adds up: The cost of VHS or a DVD-R, $3.85 for a priority stamp, and $1.50 for a puffy envelope. What if you actually do get into Sundance? The cost of the flight, the hotel, all the marketing swag, travel, press kits, the DVDs — you can fill in the blanks. If you've got a hot film on your hands, multiply it by ten, twenty, one hundred festivals."

A veteran festival attendee, Roy Unger stresses that "the festival circuit's going to eat up another year of your life. Be ready for it. Put some money aside. Budget $1,000, and that doesn't cover airfare."

HOW TO SUCCESSFULLY LAUNCH YOUR FILM

Now that you've finished with making your film, it's important to sit down and create a game plan. Think of it as a marketing plan or a launch strategy for you and your film. Ultimately, you want to be like Jeff Bemiss, who made a short called *The Book and the Rose*. "We've managed fifty-seven film festivals worldwide," reports Bemiss. "Twenty-seven awards. Academy Award semi-finalist for Best Live Action Short. We've found a boutique distributor that loves the film and has started selling it on DVD and for broadcast, premiering it recently on the two largest PBS stations in the country — WGBH Boston and KQED San Francisco." This can be you, too. If you follow the following game plan.

- *DURING EDITING, HAVE MULTIPLE PRIVATE TEST SCREENINGS BEFORE LOCKING PICTURE.*

Get feedback from people who will honestly tell you how good your film is. By the time you're ready to officially send your film out into the world, you should consider it as good as it's ever going to get.

- *MAKE POSTCARDS.*

Forget about doing posters or fancy press kits. All you need to market your film is a strong postcard.

You'll use postcards at every step of marketing your film. Make them in time to be given out at your first screening. How many postcards should you order? Most filmmakers do print orders for one to five thousand. Other filmmakers skip the formal printing and do them as needed on their computer. Whatever works for you!

- *HOLD AN INFORMAL CAST AND CREW SCREENING.*

For this screening, your film is shown on video. Preferably in an informal setting like someone's house with a big screen TV or a bar that can project video. Provide cheap food and lots of liquor. Don't worry about working the room — you are allowed to get drunk and have fun. Notify people of this screening by phone, fax or e-mail, not by postcard. Obviously, the people you're inviting are already familiar with your work and aren't an impartial audience, but this screening is your first time to see how your short plays in front of an audience. Listen to what people tell you. It's not too late to make changes before officially launching the piece.

This gathering is also a chance to have fun and celebrate everyone's achievements. When you give an introduction, your speech can be sloppy and your list of thanks elaborate. Collect everyone's e-mail address so you can send them information on the formal premiere. Have stacks of postcards to pass out so your cast and crew can invite V.I.P.s to the premiere.

- *MAKE MASS QUANTITY VHS COPIES (DVD OPTIONAL).*

Don't make multiple VHS/DVD copies of your film until after your first screening — just in case you do want to make a few minor tweaks. If you're having copies professionally done, it's cheaper to order a larger quantity at once. Don't forget to earmark copies for your cast and crew. If you figure you will be submitting to twenty film festivals, plus fielding various requests, one hundred copies will suffice. If you can afford more, make more. You'll be surprised how many you'll go through. You never want to be stingy, calling around to ask to get your tape back.

Be aware that not all festivals will accept DVD as a submission format, and not every DVD player can play DVD-Rs. Why risk it? In general, if you want to be prudent, submit VHS to festivals. However, I do sincerely believe this will change, and within a few years no one will want to deal with tapes. But for the time being, it's safer to stick with VHS.

Make sure everything — tape, box cover and spine — is labeled with your film's title and your contact information. Regarding cases, the boxes with full sleeve are nice because you can showcase your artwork. The sturdy box also adds a little more protection during mailing. Nevertheless a simple cardboard cover works just as well.

- *ASSEMBLE MAILING SUPPLIES.*

Here's something that will endear you to everyone you mail your film to: Never, ever use those jiffy padded envelopes. When those devils are opened quickly, shredded padding goes everywhere. If you want extra padding, spend a little extra to get the bubble-lined envelopes.

If you have film prints, you'll have to ship the reels when you get accepted to festivals, so get your system in place ahead of time. To get an idea of the cost of sending them priority mail, go to the post office and weigh reels packaged up. If you're worried about keeping track of your shipped print, it might be worth your while to open a FedEx account and ship using the less expensive three day service. Not only can you use their sturdy FedEx boxes, you'll avoid standing in line at the post office.

• *PUT TOGETHER A PRESS KIT AND WEB SITE.*
Press kits and web sites will be discussed in detail in the following chapter.

• *BEGIN FILM FESTIVAL SUBMISSIONS.*
As soon as you can, begin to submit to festivals because there is a lag time between the entry deadline and when your film is accepted. Your goal is to have a major festival lined up before your self-organized premiere.

The festival circuit is vitally important to the short filmmaker for many reasons. Unless you luck out and get some sort of theatrical distribution, the only time your film will play on the big screen in front of paying audiences will be at a film festival. Secondly, festivals are a priceless networking opportunity. In no other context are you so clearly identified as a filmmaker. In no other context will you meet so many other filmmakers and professionals in the film industry. Work every angle you can to meet people, make connections, and perhaps get a gig. Thirdly, buyers scout for product at festivals. If you want to sell your film to foreign television (that's where the real money is), your film needs to show at a festival where foreign buyers go. More about festivals in Chapter 16.

• *HOLD YOUR BIG PREMIERE.*
For this screening and this screening only, rent out a proper screening room. If you don't have a print, make sure the site you rent projects video at acceptable quality.

If your film is very short, consider pairing with one or two other pieces by other filmmakers. However, if you do a co-screening, make sure the other pieces are not as good as yours — you should be the filmmaker everyone fawns over! The advantages of screening with someone else are many. First, another filmmaker will have different people to invite, so the circle of V.I.P.s at your screening grows exponentially. Secondly, sharing the event helps defray the cost. Split all charges down the middle ahead of time to avoid later arguments of who had more guests attend and therefore should pay more. Lastly, people are more likely to attend if you offer more than ten minutes of programming. Guests don't want to spend more time parking their car than sitting in their seats!

Do a massive mailing for this premiere. Invite anyone and everyone who might possibly help you with your career (including press). Remember, you're a major talent who is going to go far, and they should know about you! This is the screening that officially launches you and your film. If you have an upcoming festival already scheduled, promote it with this mailing. For example, slap on a sticker saying, "Catch it now before it debuts at Slamdance in January!" This makes people think they're getting a sneak peek at a hot film. Some bigwigs won't actually make the effort to come to the screening, but they will call asking to see a copy of the film on tape. Tell them you'll mail copies after the screening.

- *AS YOU EMBARK ON THE FESTIVAL CIRCUIT, SEND POSTCARDS OR E-MAILS TO NOTIFY EVERYONE OF YOUR SUCCESS.*

"Build an e-mail list," recommends filmmaker Roy Unger. "I created a database of all the people I thought might be interested in my film. When I was having a festival screening, I would send out an e-mail sometimes before, sometimes after, sometimes both! Even if people couldn't come to my screening in Germany, they knew I was going to Germany, and when I came back, what the experience was. Invariably different people would be interested. And I said right at the bottom of the e-mail, 'If you don't want to be on this list, I can take you off very easily.' Nobody did."

Working animator Eileen O'Meara sent out missives specifically targeting companies who've hired her in the past. "Whenever I got into a few festivals, I'd send out a postcard saying 'Coming in June' and list all the festivals my film was playing, plus my name and phone number," reports O'Meara. "The idea being that a client I might not have heard from in a while would get it and go, 'I forgot about her!,' then call me up and say, 'Hello, I'd like to pay you a lot of money!'," O'Meara laughs. On a more serious note, she adds, "Also send notice of your success to any people with who helped on your film so they're glad they helped."

- *PROMOTE, PROMOTE, PROMOTE.*

Now is not the time to be shy. You've got to make a little noise to be noticed. Ari Gold, director of a very short short called *Culture*, made promotional shirts. "Selling the t-shirts, I lost money, because I gave enough away to counteract my sales," reports Gold. "But the film cost only a few hundred dollars, all the way to a print, so a few sales to TV and I was profiting. While I wouldn't neces- sarily recommend t-shirts, it was fun and added greatly to the publicity hype. I ended up being the first filmmaker being written about in the Sundance wrap-up article in the *New York Times* that year, I think in large part due to the shirts and posters. The over-promotion, for me, was a big part of the joke of hav- ing a one-shot, sixty-second film that I'd made in about two hours."

- *WIN AWARDS.*

Not every film wins awards. Of the nineteen shorts we produced at the Fox Movie Channel, a few consistently won prizes, while others never won any- thing. Obviously, the number of festivals you play increases your chances of being awarded a prize, but no one really knows what makes one film award-worthy over another. I will say, however, having been on several fes- tival juries, if the filmmaker is present at the festival and available to pick up the prize at the award ceremony, this is sometimes taken into consider- ation. If you do win an award, make sure you send a thank you note to the festival's organizers. Update your press kit and web site. And then send out a charmingly humble note to your e-mail list, thanking everyone for their belief in and support of this now award-winning film.

- *QUALIFY FOR AN OSCAR NOMINATION.*

God bless the Academy of Motion Picture Arts & Sciences. Even though there are constant debates about whether to discontinue giving awards to short films, every year short filmmakers get to accept an Academy Award on national television. While big companies like Miramax and Dreamworks spend millions on marketing their films to earn a nomination, you can qualify for one with very little effort on your part. And if you win, you can be seen on TV holding that same statue that turns major Hollywood players into blubbering fools.

Although the rules can change from year to year, there are four ways for a short filmmaker to win an Oscar. One is to win the student Academy Award. It's true, student awards aren't televised, and, even worse, the award is not the Oscar statue (it's a medal designed by Saul Bass). Still, you can claim you are an Academy-recognized filmmaker if you win one of the student awards, which also come with cash grants.

The second Academy Award category you can win is the live action narrative short film. Amazingly, only one hundred or so films qualify each year, and the Academy can nominate up to five. Those are pretty good odds! How can you qualify? Two ways. One is to win the top prize at a festival that the Academy officially recognizes (a complete list of those festivals can be found in on the *www.oscars.org* web site). The festival fills out the qualification paperwork, then you summit it with your application paperwork and film print to the Academy — all of this at no cost to you! If you don't win any of the qualifying festivals, have no fear. You can buy your way in. All you have to do is have your film screen commercially in Los Angeles or New York for three consecutive days in front of a paying audience. Of course, there are some theaters that will legitimately show your film in front of paying audiences as a real screening. But the way most filmmakers make this three-day screening happen is to pay a theater to play their film (a.k.a. four walling the theater). In Los Angeles, the Laemmle Theater makes a tidy little profit doing this. "In 2003, something like one hundred and seventeen live action films qualified for Oscar nomination," calculates Apollo Cinema's Carol Crowe, who annually books the nominated and winning Academy shorts on a nationwide theatrical tour. "Look how many short films are made a year — thousands! Many filmmakers don't realize how easy it is to qualify — that you don't have to win one of the limited qualifying festivals, that you call up a theater like Laemmle and plunk down a chunk of change — I think it's about $350 nowadays — and Laemmle will do it all for you." The Laemmle Theatre's phone number is (310) 478-1041. When I was producing shorts for the Fox Movie Channel, we did the Laemmle route for each one of our nineteen films. Consequently, all were eligible for Academy consideration. Not a single one got nominated. Just because you qualify doesn't mean you'll be a contender. The Sundance Festival winners, for example, rarely seem to get nominated. Having seen every year's Oscar selection, Carol Crowe reports, "Across the board, the live action short films seem to be very different from each other, which is refreshing. There is no rhyme or reason to the Oscars."

The other two short film Oscar categories are animated shorts and documentary shorts. Like live action, you can automatically qualify for nomination if you win an award at an Academy-recognized festival. However, the rules are different regarding qualifying via theatrical exhibition. Interested filmmakers should visit the *www.oscars.org* web site for up-to-date qualifying rules, regulations, and paperwork.

- *FIELD OFFERS FROM PEOPLE WHO SAW YOUR FILM ON THE FESTIVAL CIRCUIT.*

If your film has strong potential for Internet or TV sales, within six months on the festival circuit you should be fielding offers directly from buyers or from sales reps wanting to broker deals for you. Time to decide if you are going to rep the film yourself or have others do it for you. More about sales agents in Chapter 17.

- *SIGN WITH A SALES REP, OR DO IT YOURSELF.*
  LICENSE YOUR FILM TO INTERESTED COMPANIES.

How to make money off your short will also be covered in Chapter 17. Whether you sign with a rep or make a sale yourself, send off an e-mail notifying your fan base of these exciting new developments.

- *PUT YOUR FILM ON THE INTERNET.*

Not all shorts are festival-appropriate. Some flicks are better suited to become Internet sensations, garnering a huge following over the Web. In terms of achieving maximum eyeballs, the Internet is the way to go. "I had

260,000 people look at my film in the first four weeks it was up," marvels filmmaker Amy Talkington, whose shorts *The New Arrival* and *Our Very First Sex Tape* are on *www.Atomfilms.com*. "I got e-mails from all over the world, which was really an amazing experience." If you're going the Internet route, do an e-mail campaign sending potential viewers to your film's web address. In your e-mail, mention that you can mail VHS or DVD copies to anyone who doesn't care to watch flicks on the Internet.

One thing you should be aware of: Putting your film on the Internet can ruin other opportunities. Some festivals won't show your work if it has already played on television or the Internet. Additionally, the major television channels won't buy your film if it's been on the Internet (HBO, in particular). Academy Award consideration can also be kiboshed if your Internet debut happens before qualifying for the Oscar. If you want to play it safe, hold off Internet exhibition until after you've tested the marketplace for your short. Only after you've exhausted all other venues should you allow your film to be shown on the Web. However, once you're completely done exploiting your film, definitely make it available on the World Wide Web. Who knows what unexpected opportunities might come your way?

SHORT RECAP

- Launch yourself with your own premiere.

- Build an e-mail list and notify people of your film's continuing success.

- Playing the festival circuit should generate offers from television networks to license your film.

- If you want to win an Academy Award, make sure you read all the rules and regulations on the Oscar web site. Whatever you do, don't allow your film to be broadcast on television or over the Internet before you qualify!

- Consider the Internet the last stop on your short's exposure tour.

CHAPTER 15

PRESS KITS THAT WORK

A strong synopsis and artwork are crucial.

The truth about press kits is very few people ever see them. It's your postcard and web site that everyone who counts checks out. Those two essentials are your real press kit. But before we dive into what makes a killer postcard and web site, let's address the old-fashioned press kit.

Don't waste time making a fancy press kit. A true press kit is a working document, and those who utilize it are looking for information, not glitz. The sad fact of the matter is these kits rarely get handed to press because film journalists rarely write about shorts.

You'll give most of your press kits to festivals, which will use information contained within for their program guide. "Outside a really rare case, the press kits are dealt with my coordinator, who makes sure they're complete," says Palm Springs programmer, Thomas Harris, "and then they are filed away." Programmer Jennifer Stark agrees, "Once I've made the decision about whether to program a film, then press kits become really important. They don't help me make the decision."

You'll also give press kits to companies licensing your film for TV, DVDs, or the Internet. And that's about everyone who will ever see your press kit. No need to go overboard putting it together. Your press kit should be a few simple pages of basic information printed out from your computer and updated as needed. Put these information sheets and photos in a simple folder, which you can personalize with a copy of your postcard glued on front if you feel you must. That's it. Save your splashy stuff for your postcard, web site, and VHS/DVD case.

HOW TO MAKE A PRESS KIT

Let's run down the information you'll need for your press kit so that it will be a functional document for festivals. If you have this information in your press kit, you can simply excerpt the necessary information when filling out on-line applications or write in "see attached press kit" in the appropriate sections of an old-fashioned entry form.

• *YOUR CONTACT INFORMATION*

Specifically, your name, your credit (director, producer, etc.), e-mail, phone number, fax number, mailing address.

• *YOUR FILM'S OR YOUR OWN WEB SITE ADDRESS*

We'll cover web sites at the end of this chapter.

• *TITLE OF YOUR FILM*

The wonderful thing about short film titles (as opposed to feature film titles) is there is no fear of having one so long that it can't fit on the movie theater marquee — because short film titles never get put on marquees! Your title can be as long and as funky as you want. In fact, a unique title sparks interest. Would you want to see a fifteen-minute-long short called *I Killed My Lesbian Wife, Hung Her on a Meathook, and Now I Have a Three-Picture Deal at Disney*? Probably so. And I didn't even have to tell you that Ben Affleck directed it! Not that your title has to be a block long. It just has to be memorable. Noah Edelson's short had a main character who spent the first minute of the film jumping up and down on a manhole cover chanting "78." Noah called the piece "78." Andrew Busti and Sebastian del Castillo did a super cool experimental film consisting of faces and hands pressed against the xerox machine glass. The title *deleriouspink* (delirious intentionally spelled wrong) makes that short even more memorable.

• *LENGTH (TRT)*

This is the total running time (TRT) from the first image on screen to the last. You may want to adjust your reported TRT for various purposes. Some filmmakers subtract the running time of their credits to make their film more eligible for festival play.

- *FORMAT*

Format is tricky. It may mean what you shot on, not what your final exhibition format is. If you shot 35mm, but don't have a 35mm print, say 35mm. If you shot DV or Super-16, but bumped up to a 35mm print, say 35mm. It's always better to be 35mm!

- *ASPECT RATIO (E.G., 1:85, 1:33)*

Your film's aspect ratio matters for projection.

- *COLOR*

Whether your short is color or black and white matters for television sales.

- *SOUND (E.G., DOLBY SR)*

Another projection issue.

- *COUNTRY*

Another tricky category. If your film was shot in Israel, but you are an American and funded the film, your film's country can be either Israel or USA. Adjust to whatever works to your advantage. However, the Sundance Film Festival is definitive about how they define foreign versus domestic films: American shorts must have at least 50% U.S. financing.

- *YEAR*

This should mean year of completion, but sometimes it means year of production. In general, you want your film to be as current as possible, so the latest date you can claim is your best choice. For instance, if you shot your film in October, completed in November, but didn't start exhibiting it until January of the following year, the January date should be used as your year.

- *LOG LINE/SYNOPSIS*

Can you describe the plot in a sentence or two? That sentence-long description is known as a log line. Sometimes it's hard to boil down a complex short into one utilitarian sentence. But even the most complicated feature film has to be cut down to a one-sentence description for the listing in *TV Guide*. In fact, the *TV Guide* listing is pretty much the definition of what a log line is. Here are some examples of short film log lines from the *Short* DVD collections:

Franz Kafka's It's a Wonderful Life (Director: Peter Capaldi). Richard E. Grant stars as a tormented writer who cannot complete the first sentence of his novel.

Boundaries (Director: Greg Durbin). A desperate woman is pursued from Mexico to San Diego by a musician who pokes her relentlessly in the head with his trombone.

More (Director: Mark Osborne). An elderly inventor works on a secret project that could bring bliss to the world.

Having read these simple log lines, do you have a fairly good idea of what the films are about? More importantly, do the descriptions make you want to see the films? If so, they've done their job. Although these particular log lines don't include genre and character names, many do (e.g, "a darkly comic tale of a bank robbery gone horribly wrong." Or "Karl is a man on a mission — a mission to bring his wife to her senses."). There are no real rules about what you should and shouldn't include; if it helps to be specific, then do so. One thing you should think twice about doing is using adjectives that sound like you're praising your own film. It's okay to say "darkly comic" because that helps clarify the tone, but including descriptions like "visually ravishing" could be considered self-praise. Someone reading "visually ravishing" will immediately start judging the film — is it indeed as visually ravishing as the filmmaker claims?

Coming up with a good log line is tough. With a short, sometimes it's extremely hard to sum up the film without giving away the entire plot. Take for example, *I'm on Fire*. As you may remember from the storyboard in Chapter 7, the film begins with a shot of a house on a suburban street. All of a sudden, the front door flies open. A man completely engulfed in flames runs out. He fumbles around on the lawn like men on fire in movies always do, then flings himself into his baby blue Mustang convertible, which is parked in the driveway. Still on fire, he drives off. Still on fire, he arrives at a flower shop, buys flowers, then drives to his girlfriend's house to pick her up for a date. She opens the door to reveal she's also on fire. Obviously, fire is a metaphor for love, and the short is a comic love story. We struggled and struggled to come up with a decent log line. Finally, the filmmaker came up with the following log line: "A very short film about a guy on fire." It pretty much sums up the film without giving away the entire plot, doesn't it?

Hopefully it makes you want to watch it. Certainly it's more intriguing than my long detailed explanation of the plot, isn't it?

For feature length films, it's important to come up with a log line and also a longer synopsis. For shorts, unless your piece is a mini-feature, there's no need to create a separate synopsis. It's perfectly acceptable for your log line to function as your synopsis on any form that requests a synopsis. However, your log line does need to convey the story if it is to function as a synopsis. Some filmmakers come up with very arty log lines that they use as a synopsis. For example, for his film *Culture*, Ari Gold wrote, "This is culture." His film is only one-minute long, so you could argue there isn't much more to say. But it isn't really a plot synopsis, is it? Don't mistake taglines for log lines. Taglines are catchy attitude phrases that you will see at the end of movie trailers or on posters. For example, one of the most famous taglines ever created is "In space, no one can hear you scream." Does that line tell you what the film *Alien* is about? No. But it's a cool line that makes you want to see the film, right? Here's another cool log line — from Arayana Thomas' short *Epiphany*: "Peace by way of Hell."

While undeniably cool, taglines can't function as your log line. A log line has to answer the question, "What's your film's plot about?" "An elderly inventor works on a secret project that could bring bliss to the world" is a suitable reply. "Peace by way Of Hell" is not.

Crafting a good log line is essential because if you come up with a particularly apt one, festivals will use it in their programs. Not every festival which played *I'm on Fire* printed "a very short film about a guy on fire," but several did. Who would you rather write the description of your film — an overworked, underpaid festival flunky or you? If your log line is especially solid, everyone will repeat it practically verbatim without even thinking about it. If you were asked right now to tell someone what *I'm On Fire* is about, wouldn't you more or less parrot our wording?

There's nothing wrong with changing your log line if something strikes you as better. Many festivals will use your log line, but some will write their own. If you like theirs better, use it. Sometimes outsiders are better at crystallizing plot than filmmakers who are too close to their own work.

• *FESTIVALS/AWARDS*

Don't feel bad if you don't have any festivals or awards to list. In fact, a virginal film is more attractive to programmers who want their festival to have world premieres. By the way, you can fudge this list if you feel it will help. For example, if you get into a smaller festival first, then play a bigger one, put the biggest one first on the list. And don't include an awards category if your film hasn't won any yet.

• *CREDITS*

Credits can be reduced to just the main players, e.g., director, writer, producer, cast, DP, editor, composer, or you can print out a full listing. Whatever works best for you.

• *DIRECTOR'S BIO/FILMOGRAPHY*

Most short directors don't have other credits. Just write up a quick charming paragraph about yourself. If you have any local ties to specific film festivals, sell it in your bio ("A Park City native…").

• *OTHER BIOS*

If anyone else on your production is noteworthy, include that. "No one will know you got this incredible cast and crew, if you don't tell them," points out filmmaker Amy Talkington. "If you have elements to sell, put the information out there." In one of our Fox Movie Channel shorts, the lead dog was the pug from *Men in Black*. You better believe the dog got his own bio!

• *PRODUCTION NOTES.*

No need to do full production notes like you see in feature film press kits, but if you have anything noteworthy about your production, mention it here. Often it's impressive how many days you shot, where, etc. These are the kinds of tidbits that might intrigue someone.

Culture director Ari Gold took a unique approach to production notes. Playing off the infamous Dogme95 vows, Ari Gold created his own set of rules, which he put in his promotional material (it's even on the back of the *Culture* t-shirts):

1. The film must be exactly one minute in length.

2. The film must have no cuts.

3. The number 3 must not be mentioned.

4. The film must have live sound only (no post).

5. The film must have no dialogue.

6. Only black, white, and primary colors may be used.

7. The film must be shot in one take, with no rehearsals.

8. The film must be projected in 35mm.

9. The camera must not move.

10. Ari von Gold must perform in the film.

• *REVIEWS*

It's very hard for a short filmmaker to get reviewed, but if you do, make the most of it. Include any reviews or mentions you get in your press kit. Some filmmakers xerox the original article, others create their own quote sheet with excerpts of reviews and testimonial quotes from anyone noteworthy who ever said anything nice about their short.

• *DIALOGUE LIST (FOR FOREIGN FESTIVALS)*

For press kits going to foreign festivals, you'll need to include a dialogue list which notes every word spoken in the film and the time code when it appears. The resulting rundown is used for translations.

• *PHOTOS*

In this era of jpegs, it's incredibly easy to include a disc of images with your press kit. However, an old-fashioned black and white glossy still does the trick and has the advantage of not requiring someone to insert a disk into their computer to see what the options are. For a fairly reasonable price, you can have massive amounts of 5" x 7" glossies printed up. Or you can have an 8" x 10" done two-up, meaning two pictures per sheet, one being a killer still from the production and one being the filmmaker (you!) on set. Be liberal with your disbursement. If you've pre-sent a photo before you've even been accepted to a festival, you're miles ahead of those other film-makers who wait until their piece is officially invited to send photos. "The best piece of advice that I could give anybody," whispers filmmaker Roy

Unger, "would be get some production stills. In my particular case, I had a friend come out to my set and shoot some key images. One of those became the image that has represented *Requiem* — the *Requiem* guy in close-up. The best $40 I ever spent! It became my poster, it became my postcard. It's gone on festival flyers around the world. I've been on magazine covers and all sorts of things just because I gave them the artwork. If you give them the artwork, and it's cool, they're going to use it. It's free, they don't have to do any work." Needless to say, always label the photos on the back with your film title and your contact information because oftentimes photos get separated from press kits.

AND NOW TO THE POSTCARD

Some filmmakers print up posters for their shorts. If you have posters, festivals will display them, but they tend to get lost among the feature film posters. They also tend to disappear — as Roy Unger well knows. "I had done these really expensive *Requiem* posters. Glossy. Cost me $35 each to make," reports Unger. "I took a couple with me to a festival screening in Hamburg. When I went from one screening room to another, I realized someone had stolen one of my posters! I thought that's cool someone liked it enough to steal it and now it's probably hanging in some German kid's apartment, but that cost me $35!"

Postcards are a better investment than posters — and more multi-purpose in their uses. "The postcard is the most important thing," swears filmmaker Amy Talkington. "The postcard is everything," agrees festival programmer Thomas Harris. "That piece of art can generate validation and interest. A perception and belief system is created by what people first see — and that tends to be your postcard. It's on the outside of your press kit for the few people who get to see that. It's the thing you're mailing and handing off as your business card. If there's ever a place to spend money, it's that. This is the worst thing that I can tell any filmmaker, but the bottom line is nobody really wants to see your film. You have to create the desire in people to see it. And what ultimately opens the door first is your postcard."

HOW TO CREATE A KILLER POSTCARD

"With really inexpensive software, it's easy for anyone to make a really sharp looking postcard," declares filmmaker Karl Hirsch. "In the case of *Media Whore*, the photo was taken on a 35mm still camera, and I used Photoshop to alter the colors and create depth. It's very basic stuff. I'm not a graphic artist at all, but I've seen what movie posters look like. We made five thousand postcards. Without counting the time that it took to put it together, the actual hard cost ended up being $500 or $600. A bunch of people have now seen that image, and if they were to see it again, there would be a certain amount of recognition, and that's a really difficult thing to achieve with a tiny little movie that cost under a grand. So it was the best investment of anything we did. And it was easy. It was really easy!"

- *THE DESIGN OF IT SHOULD CONVEY THE FEEL OF YOUR MOVIE.*

"Remain true to your picture," festival programmer Thomas Harris reminds us. "Whatever your movie is, do not advertise it in a different way than what it really is all about."

- *EVERYTHING ABOUT THE POSTCARD SHOULD APPEAL TO YOUR AUDIENCE.*

Film sales agent Carol Crowe loved the postcard for *Gregor's Greatest Invention*. "I saw the postcard at a film festival here in LA, and I picked it up," recalls Crowe. "I kept looking at it and thinking I've got to call this guy because the postcard just told such an interesting story. I was pleasantly surprised to find out that the film definitely backed up what the postcard was telling. It was a great story. And it got nominated for an Academy Award. I kept telling the filmmaker how great that postcard was. He got a lot of calls from it."

- *USE A STRONG SINGLE IMAGE.*

"The way I like to do things is based on a single recognizable image or design," states marketing-savvy filmmaker Roy Unger. "It should represent the style of your movie. It should be attractive to an audience. And I think that last thing is probably the most important thing of all."

- *THE TITLE NEEDS TO BE PROMINENT.*

You need people to remember the title of the film. Don't bury it.

- *USE A TAGLINE IF YOU HAVE ONE.*

If you have a great tagline, by all means use it on your postcard (and web site). But don't worry if you can't come up with one. Very few films have great taglines. If you really want one, sometimes a line of dialogue from the film will suffice.

- *INCLUDE A BILLING BLOCK.*

Cheat off of feature posters to see how to build a block of credits at the base of your card. Note that they are usually written in a highly condensed font size.

- *PUT CRUCIAL INFORMATION ON THE BACK.*

If you want to have something printed on the back of the card, include your film's stats (i.e., USA, 35 mm, 15 minutes). Make sure your contact information is printed in a readable font. And of course, your web site address should be prominently displayed.

- *ADD STICKERS WITH RELEVANT INFORMATION.*

When you play a festival, customize your card by adding a sticker listing your screening information. This sticker can go on front or back. If you've recently won a prize, make a sticker with that information as well.

HOW TO USE YOUR POSTCARD

"Whenever we go to festivals, we give tons of postcards away," *Media Whore* filmmaker Karl Hirsch states. "We leave stacks of them at parties. We hand them out to people. Whenever we send screener cassettes, we include a postcard in the sleeve — it might as well be a full four-color video sleeve, it has the same impact. So they're useful for just about anything you'll ever need. If you make press kits, take a postcard and glue it to the front. Now you have a personalized press kit. Our film has been finished for a year and a half, and we've given out 4,995 postcards — we're all out!"

AND LAST BUT DEFINITELY NOT LEAST: YOUR WEB SITE

In the Internet age, a web site is a film's most practical press kit. "It's a way for people to reach you, it's a way for people to know more about your movie," says design guru Karl Hirsch. "Having a web presence is never bad. Besides, I don't think people know how to call information or look in phone books anymore. They go to the computer, and if you don't have a web site there's something wrong with you."

The first thing to do is register a site name. For $35 or less, you can register a domain name through various services, including Yahoo and Register.com. It's best to do the film's title, but certainly a production company or even your own name will suffice. Then put this www address on everything — including the end credits of your film. That way when your short plays on TV or on a DVD collection, people can track you down.

Your web site can be as simple as your postcard imagery and an e-mail button. Or it could be your entire press kit put on-line, including links to the festivals screening your film, reviews, stills, filmmaker's journals, etc. Always keep your web site up-to-date — you have no idea when people will see your film and want to reach you.

"I highly recommend filmmakers get a web site up, even when they're filming," declares sales rep Carol Crowe. "Get all the information up there. Put the dialogue list up. Do everything you'd do with a press kit. Instead of sending a press kit, you can tell someone go to the site, it's there."

As with any material you generate to promote your film, your web site should look professional. If you don't think you can do it yourself, think about taking a class on web site design. Or just leave the page "under construction" with nothing but your e-mail address for people to contact you. "I did the web site myself," says can-do guy Karl Hirsch. "I'm not a web designer person. I figured out how to do it because I didn't have any money to pay anyone else to do it. Learned how to do it with a program called Dreamweaver and a lot of trial and error! Because I'm not a designer I purposely made it look really simple and easy — like a bank. I found a free web hosting service. From there, I could create an e-mail address. Makes it seem like we're professionals. We constantly update the site. It is an extremely helpful tool — and essentially free."

SHORT RECAP

- When it comes to promotion, good visuals are crucial.

- Press kits are working documents. Think functional over elaborate.

- Be very liberal with your postcard distribution.

- It's never too early to establish a web presence.

- Make sure your contact information and web site address is on everything.

CHAPTER 16

PLAYING THE FESTIVAL CIRCUIT

Have the time of your life working the festival circuit.

Picture it. There you are at Sundance. Chatting with Robert Redford at the filmmakers' reception. Rubbing shoulders with Hollywood agents and studio executives at overcrowded A-list parties. And best of all,

having total strangers line up in the snow to pay money to see your little film. It could happen. It really could. All it takes is $35.

WHY YOUR IDEAL FESTIVAL CIRCUIT BEGINS WITH SUNDANCE

Everyone is familiar with the festival heavyweights: Cannes, Berlin, Venice, and Toronto. But countries like Belgium, Egypt, Finland, and Taiwan have film festivals, too. Here in the U.S., Philadelphia, Sedona, Dallas, and Fort Lauderdale are lesser known stops on the festival route. Faced with an overwhelming array of festivals to choose from, how can a filmmaker with a modest budget allocated for festival exhibition decide what's worthwhile and what's a waste of time?

The most important question to ask yourself is: What exactly do you want out of a festival experience?

• AUDIENCES APPRECIATING YOUR WORK
You made your film to be seen, didn't you? Seen by people other than your friends and family, right? Festivals are the venue where that's going to happen.

- *VALIDATION AS A FILMMAKER*

You validated yourself with your own premiere. Having a festival program-mer agree that your film is worthy of endorsement is your next major step.

- *OPPORTUNITY TO MEET PEOPLE WHO CAN FURTHER YOUR CAREER*

You want people to be so impressed by your work that they'll hire you to work for them. You might not meet these potential employers at every fes-tival, but they'll definitely be at the biggies.

- *EXHIBITION/DISTRIBUTION/LICENSING OFFERS*

If you want sales offers for your film to materialize, you need to have your work seen by acquisition executives. Such executives are trolling the festi-vals, looking for fresh meat. Make sure your film is on their radar!

- *LIFE-ENHANCING EXPERIENCES*

Also known as fun.

You can achieve all of these goals in one swoop — if you get accepted into Sundance. "The reason the Sundance shorts get seen a lot is not because they're better," points out former LA Fest programmer Thomas Harris. "It's simply the perception the festival holds that these are the best shorts." That's not to say that if you don't get into Sundance you are doomed as a failure. "I've met so many filmmakers through the years whose whole thing is about Sundance," complains AtomShockwave's director of acquisitions, Megan O'Neill. "Sundance is great. It plays a ton of short films. It's a great place for industry meetings and getting your film sold. But it's just one fes-tival. There are five thousand festivals out there. Maybe you want to be the big fish in a little pond."

Have no fear, your film can be very popular and successful on the circuit without the Redford endorsement. In fact, there are many festivals that will treat you much better than Sundance. At Aspen Shortsfest, the short film-maker is treated like a celebrity. You won't find that to be the case at Sundance (unless you really are a celebrity!).

So why should Sundance be your primary focus? Three big reasons. For films of all lengths, being an "Official Selection of the Sundance Film

Festival" means something. That brand has value in the festival world, the industry (indie and Hollywood), and the universe at large. Think about it: Even your grandmother knows what Sundance means. Sure, it's great to play the Crested Butte Reel Fest, but it doesn't really impress the neighbors, does it? Secondly, knowing that Sundance gets first crack at most films, programmers from other festivals go there to scout. You'll be surprised by the number of invitations that will come your way after your Sundance debut. When festivals solicit your film, you don't have to pay entry fees. Score! Less work, no cost! Lastly, Sundance is very good to its alumni. Your subsequent short or feature will be given special consideration by the programmers, who have already endorsed you as a Sundance-worthy filmmaker. Being in the festival can also create inroads to the Sundance Institute's writing and/or directing workshops. Your future's looking bright!

INSIDER INFORMATION ON GETTING INTO SUNDANCE

Just apply. For the 2003 festival, 3,345 shorts were submitted to the festival. Ninety were invited to screen. What was every submission's chance of getting in? You do the math. Now, of those ninety, one was directed by Richard Linklater, another by Illeana Douglas. But the majority were made by students, foreigners, first timers, and people with no inside track to the festival's programmers. "I do believe their programmers take a lot of care in their selections, and their shorts are not quite as compromised as their feature length programming is," comments festival circuit insider Thomas Harris. "I think you're given a fair spin."

So what type of shorts does Sundance program? The festival showcases an array of genres: live action, animation, documentary, experimental. "There's not a set sort of criteria as to what makes a 'Sundance short,'" explains Sundance senior programmer Trevor Groth. "We've shown everything from a minute-long film to fifty minutes, and everything in between. For me personally, as a programmer, I want a wide range — in terms of where the films are coming from, what the aesthetics are, what the themes are. If someone were to look at the entire shorts program and watch all the films, you would hopefully see a little of everything in there."

Groth adds, "People always ask me if I need world premieres for Sundance for the shorts. No. It's not like that with shorts. I would never want someone to not show their short at another film festival — just to wait for Sundance — because I think short films need to be seen in as many theaters as possible. Make the festival route. Show your film in as many festivals as possible because that's where people are going to have a chance to see your work in the format you want it to be seen." Filmmaker Amy Talkington certainly found this to be true. Her Columbia student film, *Second Skin*, played over a dozen festivals before it got into Sundance.

More good news: You don't have to have a print to play Sundance. "At the festival, in all our sections, we project both film and video," explains Groth. "For video, we have to have it transferred to a specific format, which is the Sony HD Cam."

It's only $35 to apply. What are you waiting for?

Sundance Film Festival
8857 West Olympic Blvd., Suite 200
Beverly Hills, CA 90211-3605
www.sundance.org
Tel: (310) 360-1981
Submission deadline: September
Festival: January
Notes: Don't overlook the fairly new online film festival component. Another chance to be an official Sundance selection!

AND THEN THERE'S SLAMDANCE

Slamdance is held in the same city as Sundance, at the same time of year. Although your film can't play both, you can apply to both. If you get accepted first by Slamdance, and then Sundance, congratulations! You've made a very special film that's going to do very well on the festival circuit. And don't worry, you aren't the first to pull out of the upstart in favor of the more established 'Dance.

Slamdance, in fact, has become prestigious in its own way, marketing a "more cutting edge than Sundance" angle. Doing well at Slamdance means good things will happen to you. *White Face* director Brian McDonald reports, "We went to Slamdance and won the audience award. And that helped a lot. That helped us get our film signed with Hypnotic."

Park City is such a hotbed that many satellite festivals have popped up over the years, including No Dance, Slamdunk, Lap Dance, etc. "I went to what would probably be the third tier Park City festival, Slamdunk," recalls *Requiem* director Roy Unger, "a tier below Slamdance. I won best short and best cinematography of all their films. Which was great. But more importantly, I was in Park City when it was all going on. Everybody's there. You have to go. You gotta go walk the walk."

When you network, tell people you are a filmmaker with a short screening "here in Park City." Later, when everyone goes back home, you'll remind them that you met them when your short was "playing in Park City." In their brain, "Park City" equals "Sundance;" ipso facto, you're a Sundance-associated filmmaker!

Slamdance International Film Festival
5634 Melrose Avenue
Los Angeles, CA 90038
www.slamdance.com
Tel: (323) 466-1786
Submission deadline: October
Festival: January
Notes: Slamdance puts out a DVD compilation of short films playing each year at the festival. Check out the Slamdance web site for many additional contests and activities the festival sponsors.

THE REST OF THE BEST

In addition to Sundance, there are a number of "gold standard" festivals that every short filmmaker should enter knowing if your film gets in and you win a major award, your career is set. Among the gold standard festivals: Cannes, Berlin, Venice, Rotterdam, and here in the U.S., Telluride. However, these festivals fall into the "miracle to get in" category. Not only do they accept very few shorts, the focus of these festival is certainly not on short films. Don't obsess about getting into these impossibly difficult fests. All over the world there are many other wonderful festivals, which if your film is invited to screen, many great things will happen. "Great things" can mean great treatment as a filmmaker, great audience turnout, great net-working opportunity, great prize money, or even great sales offers. You never really know where opportunity may be knocking. It's worth your while applying to a wide variety of festivals.

• NEW YORK OR LOS ANGELES-BASED FESTS

If your ultimate goal is to get industry attention, AtomShockwave executive Megan O'Neill recommends targeting festivals in New York or Los Angeles. "If you want to have the broadest number of industry people potentially see your film, you should probably focus on Los Angeles because that's where the industry is," O'Neill says. Target hip mixed festivals (features and shorts) such as the Los Angeles Film Festival or Gen Art in New York. Once your film is accepted, employ a two-prong approach to get as many meetings as possi-ble. First, notify any industry players you already know in that city that you are coming into town to attend the festival and would love to drop by their office to give them a copy of the film and tell them about your next project. On a sec-ond front, attend the fest and ruthlessly work every event, your goal being to meet additional people in the industry who can help advance your career.

• HOME COURT ADVANTAGE FESTS

While New York and Los Angeles might be tough nuts to crack, there is a place where you are pretty much guaranteed a grand hero's welcome. That place is your hometown. Always apply to festivals where you have some sort of local connection, e.g., you live, grew up, shot your film, or went to school there, etc. Although your work will be judged on its own merit, fes-tivals do like to encourage natives. It doesn't hurt that they know you'll be able to pull in an audience of friends and family. And you'll also merit press coverage way beyond what short filmmakers usually achieve. At home, you're a star with a solid fan base. Revel in it!

• DON'T FORGET FOREIGN

With domestic festivals, there is usually an entry fee to apply, and writing too many of those $35 checks can quickly deplete your marketing fund. Foreign fests, on the other hand, have the benefit of no entry fees (usually). However, if your film gets in, it's a major pain to ship your material. You will become very familiar with the multiple forms needed to export your print or tape. To avoid paying any kind of duty costs, you'll learn the magic phrase: "For cultural purposes only — no commercial value." As your film jets off to France, Brazil, and Bermuda, you'll realize your short is having a better life than you are!

• GENRE FESTS

It's easy to get lost in the shuffle of major festivals. Many a short filmmaker has been disturbed to find their work showing in the middle of a Wednesday afternoon to a near-empty theater. If you want your film to get the audience it deserves, apply to the genre festivals. Not only will your film be eagerly embraced by programmers and audiences alike, you'll get sales offers from buyers who are looking for a certain type of film and figure the genre fests are where to find them. If your short is animated, target animation-only fests, such as Annecy Festival International du Cinema d'Animation in France (you're bound to get work out of showing there). If your short is comedic, the U.S. Comedy Arts Festival in Aspen (sponsored by HBO) should be top of your list, followed by the Just for Laughs festival in Montreal. Fly yourself there and work the crowd, which will be filled with industry heavy-weights and talent scouts. Try to hook up with an agent while you're there.

If your film showcases a lesbian character, search out gay festivals such as the high profile and amazingly fun Outfest in Los Angeles. If it's kid-friend-ly, target venues such as the Chicago International Children's Film Festival. At the Fox Movie Channel, our very first short was directed by an Asian-American woman, featured an elderly character, and had a gay story line. That film was embraced by Asian festivals, women's festivals, old people festivals, and gay festivals across the world.

• STUDENT-ORIENTED FESTS

Students, you need to approach every festival with a different eye. In the first place, there are festivals that are student only. This is probably the only time in your career you'll be able to play them, so take advantage while you can. Secondly, search out festivals that offer discounted entry fees for stu-dents. Thirdly, research those fests, big and small, that have student-only award categories. In addition to the glory of graduating from film school as an award-winning filmmaker, you'll discover that the prizes (cash or dona-tions such as film stock) can really add up. If you're very successful, it's possible to finance a second short with your winnings.

- *FESTIVALS OFFERING BIG PRIZES OR CASH AWARDS*

When you're on the fence as to whether to submit to a festival or not, check to see if there are interesting prizes or cash awards being offered. The Palm Springs International Festival of Short Films, for example, offered an Emerging Filmmaker Award in 2002 that netted filmmaker Alan Brown $15,000. For Brown, it was well worth entering that festival!

- *SHORTS-ONLY FESTS*

You'll rarely find them talked about in festival roundups or guidebooks because they are beneath the radar of the feature filmmaker. But for us, shorts-only fests are major. Why? Because at mixed length gatherings, it's the features that get the lion's share of attention. This is not the case at our own fests. "You feel like the festival is about you and your work," raves *The New Arrival* director Amy Talkington. "You get the best treatment. And you make real friends." The festivals are run by really great people who love shorts. You'll be treated like an honored guest and get into the A-list parties. You'll discover the panels are full of interesting information about the short film world that you'll find incredibly helpful. With any luck, your film will be spotted by the many short film acquisitions executives in attendance. You might walk away with a licensing deal right then and there. You'll also qualify for more awards than at a mixed festival, including audience awards. You'll never regret going to a shorts-only gathering.

- *MICROCINEMAS/SHOWCASES*

Lumped in with festivals but really their own category are microcinemas and short film showcases, usually monthly screenings dedicated to exhibiting our flicks. "The showcase world, while limited, is really important," festival insider Thomas Harris points out. "Austin Film Society does short programs. There's Moxie Films in New York City. In Los Angeles, Hollywood Shorts and the American Cinematheque offer regular shorts programs, and here's the kicker: Your film gets reviewed in the *LA Weekly* and sometimes the *Los Angeles Times*. That's a big deal."

- *THE ACADEMY QUALIFIERS*

One way to qualify for Oscar consideration is to win the top prize at a festival the Academy recognizes. The list can change from year to year, so you should check with the Academy web site, but the qualifying festivals for live action and animation have included the following domestic and foreign fests.

DOMESTIC FESTIVALS:

Ann Arbor Film Festival
Aspen Shortsfest
Athens International Film Festival (note: Athens, Ohio)
Atlanta Film Festival
Austin Film Festival
Black Maria Film Festival
Chicago International Children's Film Festival
Chicago International Film Festival
Florida Film Festival
Los Angeles International Short Film Festival
Nashville Independent Film Festival
Palm Springs International Festival of Short Films
Rhode Island International Film Festival
San Francisco International Film Festival
Santa Barbara International Film Festival
Shorts International Film Festival
Slamdance Film Festival
St. Louis International Film Festival
Sundance Film Festival
USA Film Festival
World Animation Celebration (based in Los Angeles)

FOREIGN:

Annecy Festival International du Cinema d'Animation
Berlin International Film Festival
Bilbao International Festival of Documentary & Short Films
British Academy of Film and Television Arts Awards
Canadian Film Centre's Worldwide Short Film Festival in Toronto
Cannes Festival International du Film
Cartagena International Film Festival
Cinanima International Animation Film Festival
Cracow International Festival of Short Films
Foyle Film Festival

Gijon International Film Festival for Young People
Hiroshima International Animation Festival
India International Film Festival
Locarno International Film Festival
Melbourne International Film Festival
Montreal International Festival of New Cinema
Montreal World Film Festival
Oberhausen International Short Film Festival
Ottawa International Animation Festival
Siggraph
Stuttgart International Animation Festival
Sydney Film Festival
Turin International Film Festival of Young Cinema
Uppsala International Short Film Festival
Venice International Film Festival
Zagreb World Festival of Animated Films

TEN FESTS THAT WILL ROCK YOUR WORLD

If you want to make the most of your year on the circuit, here are ten essential non-Park City festivals to target.

1

CLERMONT-FERRAND SHORT FILM FESTIVAL

www.clermont-filmfest.com
Tel: (33) 04 73 91 65 73
Submission Deadline: October
Festival: January/February
Note: Megan O'Neill from AtomShockwave calls it "the Cannes of short film." By submitting your film to the festival, your work is automatically placed in the festival's market, where buyers from all over the world come to scout. "Clermont-Ferrand's where your short is going to be sold," O'Neill explains. "If it's a suitable film for foreign television, that's your best shot." The festival itself is an experience. Located in an obscure town in the middle of France, the festival brings in filmmakers from all over the world. You'll meet amazing filmmakers, see incredible films, and have a great time. Go!

2
ASPEN SHORTSFEST
www.aspenfilm.org
Tel: (970) 925-6882
Submission deadline: December
Festival: April
Note: Aspen Shortsfest is the Cadillac of American short film fests. Not only does the festival show your film in the town's ritzy Opera House to a packed audience of swells, the folks who run the festival are truly the best in the business. If you attend, you — a poor struggling filmmaker used to begging, borrowing and stealing — will find yourself in the playground of the rich, downing complimentary cocktails in Aspen's exclusive nightclubs. Don't you love the short film world?!

3
CANADIAN FILM CENTRE'S WORLDWIDE SHORT FILM
FESTIVAL IN TORONTO
www.worldwideshortfilmfest.com
Tel: (416) 445-1446
Submission deadline: March
Festival: June
Notes: A treasure to be found in the Great White North. "Canadian Film Centre's Toronto Worldwide is an excellent, very big festival," Big Film Shorts sales rep David Russell raves. "And the market is very good, too."

4
SHORT SHORTS FILM FESTIVAL: JAPAN AND LOS ANGELES
(FORMERLY KNOWN AS AMERICAN SHORT SHORTS)
www.shortshorts.org
Tel: (310) 656-9767
Submission Deadline: November
Festival: June-July
Note: "Creative Director Doug Williams and Programming Director Marliese Schneider have done a fantastic job with that festival," praises AtomShockwave's Megan O'Neill. "The press they get is absolutely amazing! Filmmakers make sales in Asia based on it. The feedback I've gotten from filmmakers is that they've been treated phenomenally."

5

PALM SPRINGS INTERNATIONAL FESTIVAL OF SHORT FILMS

www.psfilmfest.org
Tel: (760) 322-2930
Submission deadline: August
Festival: September
Note: Another shorts-only festival taking place in the playground of the rich. This one offers very generous cash prizes. Additionally, short film buyers and sales agents from all over the world come to check out the market.

6

TRIBECA FILM FESTIVAL

www.tribecafilmfestival.org
Tel: (212) 941-2400
Submission Deadline: January
Festival: May
Notes: Robert DeNiro has organized the hottest new festival around. Destined to be the new Sundance!

7

EDINBURGH INTERNATIONAL FILM FESTIVAL

www.edfilmfest.org.uk
Tel: 44(0)131 228 4051
Submission Deadline: April
Festival: August
Notes: Highly recommended by filmmakers. If you get in, go!

8

INTERNATIONAL FILM FESTIVAL CINEMA JOVE

www.gva.es/cinemajove
Tel: (34) 96 331 10 47
Submission Deadline: April
Festival: June
Notes: A Spanish festival with an amazing reputation. All the short film sales reps love it.

9
SÃO PAULO INTERNATIONAL SHORT FILM FESTIVAL
Assocation Cultural Kinoforum
www.kinoforum.org
Tel: 55 11 3034-5538
Submission deadline: June
Festival: August
Note: Who would ever have thought the Brazilians would be great patrons of the short film, but they are! Playing this hidden secret of a festival can generate Latin American sales offers. The festival programmers are also good about finding and soliciting your film.

10
CINEMATEXAS INTERNATIONAL SHORT FILM FESTIVAL
www.cinematexas.org
Tel: (512) 471- 6497
Submission deadline: June
Festival: September
Note: A wonderfully welcoming festival that recognizes live action, animation, documentary, no-budget and alternative filmmaking.

AND A FEW OTHERS
"I've heard great things about the One Reel in Seattle," lobbies David Russell of Big Film Shorts. "And the Crested Butte Reel Fest is wonderful — been there and the filmmakers are treated great." Filmmaker Amy Talkington throws in a good word for the Hamptons Film Festival and "Sedona — they bring you in and put you up." Sandrine Faucher Cassidy, Director of the Office of Festivals and Distribution for the USC School of Cinema Television, lists off a bunch of foreign fests: "Flickerfest in Australia, Tampere in Finland, and Oberhausen." Cassidy also pushes the Savannah Film Festival, which is very good to all filmmakers.

HOW TO SUCCESSFULLY SUBMIT TO FILM FESTIVALS
After submitting nineteen films to festivals all over the world, I've discovered several ways to make the process go as smoothly as possible.

• *LABEL EVERYTHING WITH YOUR CONTACT INFORMATION.*
Because your video might be separated from its box and the press kit taken apart, make sure your film's name, your name, and contact information (address, phone, fax, e-mail, web site) is on everything.

• *HAVE A FULL-TIME FAX MACHINE AND E-MAIL ADDRESS.*
Most festivals notify you of acceptance via fax or e-mail.

• *SUBMIT EARLY.*
Not only are submission fees often cheaper if you submit early, festival screening committees can get burned out by the mountain of last-minute submissions. Better to be viewed by eager eyes rather than exhausted ones!

• *YOU CAN PUSH DEADLINES IF YOU CALL.*
If you miss an entry deadline by a week or two, call the festival and ask if you can submit anyway. Because all-length festivals often program shorts last, sometimes they'll make an exception if you stress that yours is a very short film. It never hurts to ask.

• *YOU CAN GET THE FESTIVAL TO WAIVE THE ENTRY FEE
IF YOU HAVE AN ANGLE.*
If your film has won major awards, you'll get calls from festivals requesting you submit your film for their programming consideration. In this scenario, they'll offer to waive the entry fee because they're making the request. If you're the one calling them, stress that what you really want is to screen at their festival; unfortunately, you've already exceeded your budget for festival submissions, and you can't afford their fee. At worst, you might get them to discount their fee. Your best angle, however, is if you've previously made a short that played that particular festival in past years. You then call, explaining you had such a great experience last time that you desperately want your new film to be considered; unfortunately, you're on a much stricter budget this year. See if they bite.

• *SEND PHOTOS WITH YOUR APPLICATION.*
Festivals need artwork for catalogue and press purposes almost immediately after locking programming. If the fest already has your photo, there's a very good chance your image will be used.

- *LIE ON YOUR APPLICATION.*

Filmmakers lie. If you think it will help your chances of getting in, stretch the truth about your running time, if your film already had its world premiere, if it's been on the Internet or TV, if you have festival clearance for your music, etc.

- *DON'T GIVE UP IF YOU DON'T GET IN TO THE FIRST FEW FESTIVALS YOU ENTER.*

It's a matter of getting through the nos until you get the yes. Persevere. Take inspiration from Douglas Horn's experience. "My short, *Trailer: The Movie!*, has enjoyed a very respectable run to date," states Horn. "It has been an official selection in twenty festivals, has received multiple distribution offers (which I'm currently deciding between) and has played in independent theaters before feature films (for pay, no less). Along the way, it garnered some very positive reviews. Not bad for a film that took six months to get its first festival acceptance!"

- *INFORM FESTIVALS THAT YOU'VE APPLIED TO OF RECENT MAJOR DEVELOPMENTS. INFORM THOSE ON YOUR E-MAIL LIST AS WELL.*

If you get into Sundance after you've already applied to other festivals, send the festivals a quick fax notifying them of your new status. Programmers do track hot flicks, and they'll be even more interested in your short now. Festival insider Thomas Harris also suggests you share news of your acceptances far and wide. "The bottom line with launching a short is after you've premiered, you need to allow the film industry to understand that your short is moving out — that it's everywhere they turn. That's why it's really important to be notifying them as your film plays other festivals so they can start to see that it's not a one-shot wonder that played Cleveland but was never heard from again so why should they watch it? No, no, no, it started at Cleveland, now it's playing the Los Angeles Film Festival, and it was at the Boston Film Festival last week. It is very important to create the perception that your short has legs, and it's everywhere."

- *CONSIDER USING A PROFESSIONAL SUBMISSION SERVICE.*

If the idea of keeping track of deadlines and re-filling out the same information on entry form after entry form drives you crazy, you might want to look into a service like Without a Box (*www.withoutabox.com*), which can handle all the submission paperwork for you. Many filmmakers swear by it.

- *ONCE YOUR FILM IS ACCEPTED, HAVE THE PREVIOUS FESTIVAL SHIP YOUR PRINT TO THE NEXT FESTIVAL FOR YOU.*

While most festivals will not pay to have your print shipped to them, they will pay to return your print after the screening. A good way to save shipping fees is to have the festival forward your print to your next scheduled festival. If you can keep the chain going, you'll never have to pay another shipping fee.

HOW TO SCORE A FREE TRIP TO A FILM FESTIVAL

Your film gets into the fun and funky South by Southwest Film Festival. Where would you rather be: in Austin watching audiences experience your film for the first time — or sitting at home watching *Barton Fink* on the Independent Film Channel for the fifth time? It's always better to be there. Unfortunately, most festivals do not cover travel and lodging for short filmmakers. Fortunately, short filmmakers are used to begging for free stuff. Call the festival and ask to speak to the person in charge of arranging travel for filmmakers. One filmmaker I know talked a festival into putting her on a panel so her trip could be covered by the budget for panelists. Another offered to make airport runs and usher at screenings in exchange for volunteer lodging. If there's anything you have learned in your career as a short filmmaker, there's always an angle that can be worked.

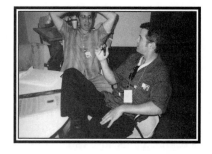

MOST IMPORTANTLY: HAVE FUN

Filmmaker Roy Unger still rhapsodizes about his time at Hamburg. "They hosted these dinners every night," Unger smiles. "Totally comped.

Filmmakers from around the world. Peter Greenaway was there. Jim Jarmusch. I met the Polish brothers. People whom I would never have access to, just hanging out at dinner, eating, drinking, and talking film."

Circuit vet David Birdsell also enjoyed his festival experiences. "See a lot of films while you're there," recommends Birdsell. "See what other people are doing. Meet other filmmakers. Get a sense that you're not alone out there. The thing that always inspires me about Clermont-Ferrand is seeing how much short filmmaking is going on all over the world right now as we speak. How many different things are being tried. I wouldn't spend thousands of dollars traveling all over the world, because you don't generally go to a film festival and come back with some sort of film deal. But if you can go, it's great because you feel legitimized and encouraged."

SHORT RECAP

- In planning your ideal festival circuit, make Sundance your main objective.

- Even if you don't get into Sundance, go to Park City for networking opportunities.

- Playing foreign festivals can trigger foreign television licensing offers.

- Target festivals offering cash-based awards. You can earn thousands of dollars on the festival circuit.

- Short-centric festivals will be your best festival-going experience. Enjoy them!

CHAPTER 17

HOW TO GET RICH OFF YOUR SHORT

Sadly, most short films don't earn back enough money to break even.

If you made your short with the idea that you were going to sell it for big bucks and retire, I have bad news for you. While it's true a very lucky few can earn beaucoup bucks off their films, the majority of filmmakers dream of breaking even. The reality is most

operate at a loss. Especially when you add in the time personally invested.

How you're going to get rich is selling yourself — using your short to achieve a career that makes you a lot of money. The short is an investment. It's a demonstration of what you can do as a filmmaker. That's why shorts are often called "calling cards" — they represent you and your talents.

"How many people go into short films thinking they're going to be making a lot of money?" laughs John Halacky of IFILM. "They're going into it for exposure, for the calling card aspect, for getting something done, getting out there, getting their name known. And that's what they should be doing. A short can be a stepping stone for a bigger and better career in filmmaking."

You're not going to get rich, but you can recoup some cash — if your film has nothing that will prevent it from being copied, exhibited, distributed, and exploited in a commercial vein. Potential distributors will ask you if your film has all clearances and rights for commercial distribution. Do not lie about this. You're now entering a professional arena involving contracts, money changing hands, and potential lawsuits; you're expected to behave like a responsible professional studio as opposed to a flighty artist. What could happen if you lie? The offended parties could demand an injunction, stopping your film from being exploited. That's what happened with Todd Haynes and

Superstar. Richard Carpenter didn't find the unlicensed use of his music and slanderous portrayal of his character very amusing. Consequently, you'll never find Haynes' film commercially distributed. Even worse, you could be required to pay damages. Of course, the resulting publicity can be a boost to your profile. But do you want to be known throughout the industry as the filmmaker that pissed off Richard Carpenter? The fact is, if you're attempting to make money off your short, your work does have value and you should be taken to task like anyone else making a commercial product.

"If you want your film to be sold — and I've never met a filmmaker who afterwards didn't want their film to be sold — do not use music you haven't paid for," adds AtomShockwave director of acquisitions, Megan O'Neill. Distributors will also ask if your project was produced under any guild or union agreements with any potential distribution issues. If you signed a SAG contract stipulating you must pay all your actors their SAG fees in full the moment your film earns one penny, you might not be able to accept sales offers too small to cover your SAG bill.

SO HOW MUCH CAN YOU MAKE?

Let's cut to the chase and ask sales reps from the major short film distributors exactly how much money a short film could potentially rake in.

Andrew Weiner, former Senior Director of Acquisitions and Development for Hypnotic: "How much can you get for a licensing, say, a ten minute piece? The answer is sometimes not a lot, sometimes a tremendous amount. It really depends. Some films turn into phenoms where they're licensing to tons and tons of territories, and they're fetching a fairly high value for them. Then other films are truly fantastic but generate next to no revenue."

Megan O'Neill of AtomShockwave: "It really depends on the film. There are filmmakers who have probably seen tens of thousands of dollars and a rare few who have done amazingly well have seen maybe one hundred grand over time. I'm a little skeptical that people could see more than that — and definitely that is not the norm. Most filmmakers, I would say, over the length of their film distribution, would see thousands, maybe tens of thousands. In the low tens. If the film has done fairly well. And if it's more than five minutes long. Because a lot of the television stations pay by the minute. That's the Catch-22. There are still a lot of places that are paying by the minute."

David Russell of Big Film Shorts: "What the average film gets is around $5,000, and that's selling to multiple markets worldwide. Such low numbers are not the film's fault or a reflection of its appeal. No one who buys shorts pays very much, except for aberrations like HBO, and they buy very few films."

Carol Crowe of Apollo Cinema: "Not every short out there is going to sell. Remember that. Every year there is going to be that handful that you will continually see on the festival circuit. And those are the ones that most of the buyers are interested in. Frankly, shorts are so hit or miss. I would say just to be safe, if you're lucky, an average film will earn five grand."

The important thing to remember is you're not selling your film just for the money, but for the exposure. Filmmaker Roy Unger licensed his film to the Sci Fi Channel. The problem was the money wasn't great. "As I made the festival circuit, I was getting offers, it's just that none of the offers were good," Unger recalls. "The Sci Fi thing was an offer to get it on television. Everything else was an offer to stream it, or this or that. This Sci Fi thing was a crappy deal, but it was a hot show for a filmmaker to get their stuff seen. So I made the deal with the help of a lawyer, whom I had look at the contract, and his fees ate up a third of what I made! But I had to protect myself; I didn't want to sign something giving Sci Fi Channel rights to exploit me. I got my film on air, and within days I had people calling me and I got meetings. More people saw my film on one night on cable television than ever saw it in all thirty-four film festivals around the world."

MARKETS TO EXPLOIT
Unlike features, which have a set flow of windows, shorts can be exploited in all markets at all times.

• THEATRICAL
It's almost impossible to get paid to show your film in commercial theaters, but Big Film Shorts distributor David Russell is making headway with the Regal Cinema chain. Carol Crowe's Apollo Cinema has done quite well with annual nationwide tours of the Academy-nominated shorts. And animators Don Hertzfeldt (*Rejected*) and Mike Judge (*Beavis and Butt-Head, King of the Hill*) are also making inroads with an ambitious theatrical tour called

The Animation Show, a collection of the world's best animated short films, personally programmed by Hertzfeldt and Judge. The guys said in their official announcement, "As animation continues to be plagued as the single most misunderstood film medium, the animated short film is sadly under-valued and underexposed in American cinema, despite widespread appre-ciation throughout the rest of the world. With luck, popular animated shorts may see some manner of very limited theatrical play, but are all too often relegated to only being found in chopped-up form on television, or worse, are only exhibited on the Internet. Every year, The Animation Show prom-ises to put animated short films into more theaters than any other anima-tion festival in American history. We aim to finally give these filmmakers the wide exposure their work deserves and to share these short master-pieces on the big screen, where they belong."

- *NON-THEATRICAL*

Non-theatrical opportunities include schools, colleges, libraries, military institutions, prisons, museums, churches, etc. Short docs, in particular, can earn good money licensed to these organizations.

- *TELEVISION — DOMESTIC AND FOREIGN*

Licensing to television is where the bulk of your money will be made. In general, it's the long-established foreign television channels, such as France's Canal+, which will pay the biggest licensing fees (paying by the minute). In the U.S., HBO is the gold mine — paying up to $1,000 a minute — but the channel doesn't acquire many shorts. A more realistic domestic television sale is to the Sundance Channel or the Independent Film Channel for a flat fee, usually a couple of thousand. With the explosion of digital cable and satellite, more and more channels will be created, which means more potential opportunities. The first shorts-only channel, Movieola, was launched in Canada in 2001, and similar networks are bound to pop up all over the world.

- *AIRLINES*

Some sales reps have great relationships with airlines and can license your film to many carriers for fairly good money. On your own, you'll find it hard to make these sales.

• *VIDEOGRAM — VHS/DVD, CD-ROM, ETC.*

Because DVD is the perfect format for short film compilations, new DVD series are constantly being launched. Unfortunately, most of these commercial compilations do not generate any real money (never expect to see a penny of any promised royalties), but they do offer exposure. If individuals approach you about putting your short on their compilation, there's no reason to grant them exclusive DVD rights. If it's exposure you're looking for, make non-exclusive deals with as many DVD companies as possible.

If you want to sell a short yourself, you might want to look into the Amazon Advantage program. If Amazon finds your film acceptable (they take one or two weeks to review any material you submit), you'll ship consignment copies to the Amazon warehouse and get a listing on the site. Before Amazon can sell it, you have to secure a bar code for the packaging (you can get a Universal Product Code from *www.uc-council.org*). When people buy your DVD via Amazon, the company will ship it within 24 hours, just like a "real" movie. The cost to you is an annual enrollment fee of $29.95, and Amazon takes a 55% commission on all sales.

Another way to go is to use a company like CustomFlix. You send CustomFlix your video, and they transfer it to DVD, set up a customized sales page, handle e-commerce, on-demand duplication, and order fulfillment. They take care of credit card processing and send you monthly profit checks. The service costs as little as $50 to use if you've already authored a DVD, or $99 and up if you have a videotape. It's a lot less work than trying to do everything yourself. "CustomFlix launched a new 'Indie Shorts' service in Fall 2003," reports company rep Darren Giles, "with the goal of revolutionizing the distribution of independent short film. Historically, it has been very difficult to find distribution opportunities for short films. With this new initiative, short filmmakers send in their films, which are added to the CustomFlix Indie Shorts collection. The collection is marketed to the public audience, who can then browse the collection and select whichever set of shorts catch their eye. CustomFlix produces and sells these custom compilations and pays the filmmaker a royalty per sale. This is a unique way to get your film in front of potential viewers, and is definitely worth checking out." For more information on CustomFlix, check out their web site (*www.CustomFlix.com*).

• *INTERNET/NEW DEVICES*

During the dot-com era, many companies were built on the belief that new technology would be a gold mine. AtomShockwave, in particular, preached that short films would be shown on cell phones, palm pilots, gas station pumps, ATMs, etc. That hasn't really happened yet, but it still might. As it now stands, the Internet is the only new platform that has really paid off. If your short is Internet-friendly, you'll get all sorts of offers to show it on various sites. Sometimes there's money involved, other times it's free streaming. "As a distributor, I say try to get some money out of it," counsels sales rep Carole Crowe. "But otherwise, you are getting exposure, which can translate into a dollar figure at some point." If the name of the game is exposure, why not say yes? One reason to hesitate: some television networks won't take your short if it has been on the Internet. Keeping in mind that the most lucrative market for shorts is television, why jeopardize this revenue stream by putting your film on the Internet without any financial gain?

HOW TO GENERATE OFFERS

Play the festival circuit. This is where sales reps and the buyers scout for material. If offers don't come to you via festival exposure, you can contact the buyers directly. Most television channels have a fairly quick evaluation process, usually forty-five to ninety days. Do not call to follow up during that time period. Of course, a postcard or an e-mail with a news update wouldn't hurt. Most cable networks and Internet companies do keep records, so don't resubmit if you have officially been passed on. Seek other opportunities. Remember, it's just a matter of getting through the nos until you get a yes.

HIRING A PRO

If offers come to you, you can either accept the deals and sell the film yourself, or you can sign with a sales rep or distributor who will broker deals for you. "It's all about the relationships," points out filmmaker Amy Talkington. "How are you going to track down and get someone from Canal+ on the phone? Ideally the rep has relationships with all the foreign television networks and venues you aren't even aware of, like airlines or Internet deals. Reps know what windows to do first so you don't mess up other possibilities. Also it gives you that experience of working with an agent, a professional relationship similar to what you hope to have in the future."

Carol Crowe, a sales rep from Apollo Cinema, adds, "The advantage of going with a film rep, distributor, or sales agent is that we can do the job while you've moved on to doing other things. You should be busy getting your feature going, not still working your short. Without a doubt, you can sell your film yourself. But it can be time consuming, and it can feel daunting looking at legal agreements. Some filmmakers want to show licensing agreements to an attorney. If you show it to an attorney, right there it's cheaper to go with a sales agent."

How do you get a sales agent? Like buyers, they cruise the festival circuit looking for hot films they think they can sell. Remember, they're not representing your career, they're representing a property which they'll exploit for both your and their profit. If no sales reps contact you, you can contact them. Doing a Google search will turn up a listing of potential short film sales agents.

Agreements with reps vary. Some offer an advance against future earnings. Some take a percentage of whatever deals they broker. When you sign with a sales rep, you will sign an agreement that will cover the following:

- *GRANT OF RIGHTS*
You do not need to have the rep handle all rights. If you've already sold your film to certain markets on your own, those can be excluded from the agreement. Or you can split the film's rights to have a North American rep and a European rep.

- *DISTRIBUTOR'S CREDIT*
Some sales agents who also act as distributors will insist their logo be placed on your film. This isn't necessarily a bad thing, but be aware that it is an issue that should be clarified.

- *COMMISSION*
It can range anywhere from 30% to 70% in some markets. While such large percentages may sound like a lot, sometimes the amounts being earned are less than $100. If your rep is covering costs out of their take, a sizable percentage isn't unreasonable.

- *EXPENSES*

This is another element that varies. Are you being charged for phone calls, faxing, shipping, tape duplications, etc? Make sure it is spelled out in your agreement what the agent/distributor can charge back against any monies generated by the film. See if there's any wiggle room. Because you're probably a better bargain hunter than they are, offer to provide screening dubs, clones of your master, copies of your press kit, etc.

- *PAYMENT*

Some reps will pay you as soon as they get a check in hand, others will report quarterly, semi-annually or even annually. Remember, a big part of the representative's job is getting money for you — but it does take time to get checks from the companies they license to.

- *LENGTH OF AGREEMENT*

Make sure it's clear how long your deal will exist and how you can break the relationship if you aren't pleased with the results.

SELLING YOUR FILM YOURSELF

The first thing you need to know is the word sell is misleading. You should never sell your film outright. Exhibitors pay you a fee to license your film for an agreed-upon period of time for a specific medium and territory. For example, you might say you sold your film to the Sundance Channel, but the reality is the Sundance Channel licensed your film for two years exclusive domestic television for $1,500.

When you make a deal, you will be asked to "represent and warrant" that you have the exclusive right to use and grant rights to the film and hold the licensing company harmless of any and all negligence in connection with your film. And because television channels will make payments to the composer's organization (BMI, ASCAP, SESAC), a music cue sheet will be required.

When the deal is finalized, you will be required to deliver a master. This is not your real master, but a clone of it that you will give to the company for the duration of their licensing. The most preferred format for delivery is DigiBeta.

Many cable channels will also ask for a standard set of deliverables. Features must have everything, but it's perfectly acceptable for you to say,

"It's just a short film, I don't have that material." For example, you may be asked to deliver:

- *COLOR TRANSPARENCIES (SLIDES) OR SETS OF PRINT STILLS*

See if you can substitute jpegs.

- *POSTERS*

Try to substitute your postcard.

- *TRAILER*

Inquire if they really need this for a film as short as yours.

- *A CLOSED CAPTIONED VERSION*

Offer up your dialogue list instead. If they insist, ask for a bigger licensing fee to cover the cost of making a closed caption version.

- *M & E (MUSIC AND EFFECTS) TRACK*

This is a dialogue-less version of your film for foreign television. Most short filmmakers do not have such a version. Offer up your dialogue list for sub-titled translation.

- *E & O (ERRORS AND OMISSIONS) INSURANCE*

Most short films don't have E&O insurance, which is very expensive. Luckily, the cable or DVD companies requiring E&O usually offer a bigger licensing fee to cover the policy coverage cost. If this isn't the case, offer to sign whatever legal forms the acquiring company wants you to sign to indemnify them against any possible errors and omissions.

DEALING WITH CONTRACTS

You can hire a lawyer to look over any contracts you might be offered, but in general the biggest, most reputable companies like HBO or Canal+ in France will offer you a boilerplate contract which they will not be willing to change. Don't be intimidated by the paperwork. Most acquisition deals are very straightforward. The basic elements in a licensing contract will generally include:

- *DESCRIPTION OF THE CONTENT, INCLUDING RUNNING TIME*

Do not lie about your running time when it comes to licensing. Your running time must be exact, in minutes and seconds. Some television channels or DVD companies pay by the minute.

- *THE TERRITORY COVERED BY THE AGREEMENT*

It can be just a specific area (U.S. and Canada, for example) or it could be the world.

- *TERM*

The contract should spell out exactly when the agreement begins and when it terminates. It could be for a limited window (a few months or a few years) or in perpetuity. In general, you should be wary of long contracts.

- *RIGHTS GRANTED*

Is it exclusive (meaning you can't license it elsewhere) or nonexclusive? What media does it cover? Some TV channels, for example, are now asking for Internet rights as well.

- *DELIVERY INFORMATION*

Exactly when and how you should deliver your master and other required materials should be spelled out.

- *LICENSOR WARRANTIES*

This is where you must make your guarantees that everything is on the up and up. It usually includes statements that you are the sole owner of the copyright, there is no agreement with someone else that will interfere with the rights you granted, the content is free and clear of any encumbrances, and that you will make all necessary talent, production, royalty, union, and other such payments. You are usually required to indemnify the licensing company against any claims or lawsuits that might develop.

- *PAYMENT SCHEDULE*

Some licensing deals are royalty-oriented. Other companies will pay you part of the licensing fee upon signing the contract and the rest when your short first airs or is first put in stores (in the case of DVDs). Ideally, you'd want 100% of the license fee payable upon receipt and technical acceptance of the delivery materials.

THINGS TO WATCH OUT FOR

When reviewing contracts, keep an eye out for the following issues:

- *IF THE LICENSOR FINDS THE MATERIAL DEFECTIVE, INCOMPLETE, OR UNACCEPTABLE*

For example, what happens if your master is rejected for not being of acceptable broadcast quality? It might not be financially worth your while to bring your material up to acceptable standards. Look for an out-clause, making the contract null and void if this happens.

- *EDITING RIGHTS*

Filmmakers usually freak out about this. But often editing means a TV network will squeeze your film's end credits or run them at the end of a compilation program of short films. Rarely are shorts edited for content.

- *ASSIGNMENT OF GRANTED RIGHTS TO OTHERS*

Assignment was an especially touchy issue in the era of the dot-com implosions. When companies license shorts, the films become company assets that can be traded, sold, or "assigned" to other companies as long as the license period lasts. You may sign up with one DVD company, only to find they've gone out of business and sold to someone else. You can ask to have this clause stricken from the contract, but most companies won't go for it. If nothing else, ask for the agreement to become null and void if the company declares bankruptcy. Many short films have been tied up in long contracts with companies that have gone bust.

- *PAYMENT PROCEDURES*

Check to see if you need to send an invoice to get paid. If so, make sure you keep your eye on the calendar and submit invoices promptly. An invoice can be a simple memo from you to the company requesting payment. Make sure you include an invoice number at the top of the memo (corporations are used to dealing with invoice numbers).

THREE ESSENTIAL NEGOTIATING TERMS

You just want to make money, not be a lawyer. Don't be intimidated by the process. You can survive contract negotiations by knowing three magic words.

1

"FEE"

You don't pay the licensing fee. They do. Unfortunately, a lot of the fees you will be offered, especially for Internet or DVD compilations, will be "gratis." Always insist on some sort of nominal fee — if only to cover costs of making a master and shipping it to them.

2

"NONEXCLUSIVE"

Nonexclusive means you can license your film again and again in the same market — no one can have the exclusive right to it. "Be aware once you sign your first nonexclusive agreement for that right, you can never go back and do an exclusive anywhere," cautions sales agent and distributor David Russell of Big Film Shorts. "This can be a problem for some broadcasters. Once you've gone to the broadcasters who are exclusive, then you're free to do all the non-exclusives. All PBS stations are nonexclusive, for example. So start with broadcasters that are exclusive. Simultaneously, you can do DVD, airlines, all the other markets because they don't conflict and there isn't the order of windows like there is with features."

3

"NO"

"Don't be afraid to say no," film sales agent Carol Crowe counsels filmmakers. "That's the key thing in shorts. Everyone's always afraid when they get an offer — 'I better do it, I better do it.' But it's okay to say no. It's okay to walk away. Everyone wants your films for free, whether it's the Internet or whatever. I just don't think you should give something for free. You worked so hard and all your money's in there. My big thing I say to every filmmaker is: You are worth your wage!"

MORE MONEY

A decade ago no one had heard of DVDs or palm pilots. Who really knows what tomorrow's technological innovations will be? Who knows what new licensing opportunities will develop? As a studio, you must consider your short an asset to be continually exploited. Spread the distribution of your film as wide as possible and embrace every opportunity that comes your way. Take a page from Mark Osborne's *More* playbook. "*More* keeps selling," exclaims sales agent Carol Crowe. "He keeps breathing more and more life in it." Just when it seemed as if every possible venue for *More* had been exploited, Osborne recut it and got it played as a music video on MTV2. In a few years time when everyone will be watching shorts on cell phones, *More* will be undoubtedly playing there, too.

SHORT RECAP

- While an extremely successful short film might generate tens of thousands in licensing fees over a period of years, most shorts are lucky to score $5,000 total.

- Always read contracts carefully.

- Try for nonexclusive deals.

- Don't be afraid to say no.

- New markets will always open up, extending the life of your film.

CHAPTER 18

PARLAYING YOUR LITTLE FILM INTO A BIG CAREER

Always have something you want to do next.

Here's the dream version: An important agent, an indie film maven, a Hollywood studio exec, a high-profile ad guy, a music video production company owner — you fill in the blank — catches your short film at a festival (or a screening) and instantly realizes they must give you loads of money to

make fabulous things for them. In reality, this does happen. Short film-makers pay off their credit card debt with the obscene fees they earned shooting Budweiser or Burger King commercials. NYU graduates turn their thesis shorts into features shown in mall multiplexes across America (in Peter Sollett's case, it was expanding the half-hour _Five Feet High and Rising_ into the feature-length _Raising Victor Vargas_). "It's not that that isn't going to happen," sighs short film distributor David Russell, "it just doesn't happen all the time."

When you step out beyond the short film world, you'll discover that potential employers aren't interested in your short as a piece of valuable property. Their interest lies in you — and what you can do for them. To make the next step, short filmmakers must have skills and/or future projects that agents, indie film mavens, Hollywood studio execs, high-profile ad guys, music video production company owners — you fill in the blank — will find interesting and, most importantly, potentially profitable.

How can you impress these future employers? "Some filmmakers fall into the trap of making a short that looks exactly structurally like episodic television comedy," remarks former Palm Springs programmer Jennifer Stark. "Even though in theory that shows that you can handle that type of directing assignment, that's not going to sell you to Hollywood. What sells filmmakers is presenting something completely unique that catches people's attention. It's hard because on one hand you're creating a calling card to demonstrate your technique. But on the other hand, the director whose talent is going to spark interest is somebody who is doing something different."

Megan O'Neill of AtomShockwave pinpoints a director who was able to parlay her short into a very successful directing career. "I think a really good example is Kim Peirce, who went on to direct *Boys Don't Cry*," says O'Neill. "Years ago she made a terrific short film in which she had two Frank Sinatra songs. The songs fit the film perfectly. Just exquisite. I called her saying, 'Would you ever consider changing that music to sell the film?' She said, 'No, I really wouldn't. I don't want to sell it. I just did it because this was the story I wanted to tell.' I thought, 'Good for you!' Her film was so good that you knew she was going to make it. You knew she was going to get a shot because it was original, it was personal, it had a vision, and it didn't really matter if it sold or not. I think that Kim Peirce made it because she had that vision, and she knew what she wanted to accomplish."

Festival programmer Thomas Harris agrees. "If you can create a compelling character — an all-out original three-dimensional human being — or you can capture an emotional honesty on screen in a short film capacity, you will turn heads really fast," Harris swears. "I firmly believe if you do that, you'll find doors opening to you. It may not be a deal at Paramount or Universal. But it might very well be somebody who can lead you to some financing for your feature, or maybe for your next short, or whatever it is you want to do." Harris adds, "The best way to have good fortune is to have a short that is really well liked on the festival circuit, and at the same time that that's happening, have a feature film script underneath your arm ready to go."

Lexi Alexander, who found herself being wined and dined after her short *Johnny Flynton* was nominated for an Oscar, played it smart. "I have met with pretty much every executive in town," she explains. "There have been several scripts offered to me to direct, but I have been holding off to set up my own script. It now has found a home, and I am excited to make my feature debut with a subject that is dear to my heart."

HOW TO LAND YOUR DREAM JOB

"A lot of filmmakers think once you start the festival circuit, everything's going to come to you," observes Burbank-based sales agent David Russell. "The thing filmmakers need to know is once you've made your short, that truly is just the beginning. It's up to you to get to New York or Hollywood. It's up to you to get the meetings. You can't stay out of the loop, just hoping that having made a film is enough to change your life. You need to use your short as a tool for getting your career kickstarted. And no one can do that better than you. I tell filmmakers, 'I don't represent your career, I represent your film. If you want a career, you better get here and start it. And a short film can help it.'"

So what kind of career do you want to kickstart?

• *FEATURE FILM DIRECTOR/SCREENWRITER*

If your goal is features, have projects ready to go. When you attend festivals, ruthlessly work the crowd. Meet and talk to anyone associated with feature films. Ask other directors you encounter for advice. See if you can get them to introduce you to their agent or their producer. Referrals are invaluable. "When you get that friendly in," stresses director Mat Fuller, "it's like the difference between going to a job interview that your buddy hooked you up with and one where you don't know anybody."

Of course, getting meetings is much easier if you have an agent. If you're lucky enough to have a hot film, agents and managers will seek you out. "My agent came through a screening my school did in Los Angeles," reveals Columbia grad Amy Talkington. "An agent from UTA came and said, 'I think this new agent here would really like your work.' I had interest from three or four agents, but I wanted to wait until I had a feature script because I wanted to make sure I was on the same page completely with someone."

Making sure you and your new "team" have the same game plan is crucial. "When I won at Sundance, lots of agents and managers suddenly wanted to talk to me, wanted to know what I wanted to do next," remembers *More* director Mark Osborne. "That same weekend was when I found out my film was short-listed for the Academy Award. It wasn't until two weeks later that we knew we were nominated. That period of time was insane. Once the nomination came through, that was a whole other realm of calls from agents and managers. I knew nothing about the industry. The world of agents and mangers and going to the next level was something that I was not really prepared for and didn't know anything about. It's funny because I definitely had my foot in the door, but I didn't have my next project figured out. I had a live action project that my brother and I had been developing for years, sort of our pet project. But that was a difficult step to take because I had a lot of heat as an animation director. If I had jumped right from there to music videos, I probably would have had an easier time. But what I did was get independent money and make the live action feature. I ended up signing with ICM, which turned out to be a mistake. ICM just wanted to say they had another Academy-nominated guy. I think they just wanted to rep me just in case I won. And when I didn't win, it was like 'Oh, well….' They're okay guys. They're all just trying to make a buck. They didn't know what to do with me. What was problematic was I wasn't meeting people because of the work, I was meeting people because of the accolades. It took me a while to figure that out. You know, I always felt that I needed an agent or manager to get somewhere. And when I just went ahead and made my film, they all wanted to talk to me. I still don't understand — there's no magic solution. I don't have an agent or a manager now. And I got my own job at Dreamworks without an agent or manager. I got my own job just for doing work. I see having an agent or manager as relatively unimportant. It's the work that matters. If you feel like you need somebody to help you find the right projects or whatever, then that's something to look into. But find somebody you connect with. And remember all they care about is the money."

• FEATURE DOCUMENTARY OR ANIMATOR

For documentary filmmakers, it's important to have projects and proposals ready to go. As you meet people during the festival circuit, seek out information about funding opportunities. For animators, your route is most likely the studio system. In the old days, Cal Arts was considered a farm team for Disney. Now it's Dreamworks, Pixar, and the CGI companies cruising the student showcases, snapping up new talent. You might not get to direct your own feature, but you'll definitely work.

- *TV WRITER/DIRECTOR*

If you want to be hired on to an existing show, you'll want to get an agent who can send you out on meetings. If you want to pitch a new show, hook up with an established production company. Karl Hirsch got an option deal with Broadway Video to develop his short, *Media Whore*, into a TV show. "I happened to meet a marketing guy who works for Broadway Video," recalls Hirsch. "We were just sort of talking. He said, 'What else is going on?' I told him that I had just done a film, and I gave him the *Media Whore* postcard. And he said, 'Wow, this looks really good. I'd love to see it.' Then I added, 'We have this whole TV show pitch based on the film.' With Broadway, we pitched the show to Fox, E! Entertainment, and Comedy Central. So even though nothing happened, I got to meet all these network people. And it wasn't like I met them saying, 'Can I please work in your mailroom?' It was more like 'Hey, I'm a legitimate producer!'"

- *MUSIC VIDEO DIRECTOR*

Make a visually interesting short with a strong music video sensibility. "I've shown shorts to people who have ended up hiring those filmmakers to make videos at Sub Pop Records for $10,000," proclaims formerly Seattle-based short film exhibitor Joel S. Bachar. "So those opportunities do exist."

- *COMMERCIAL DIRECTOR*

Ad execs frequently attend festivals trolling for new talent. Short filmmakers who aspire to enter the world of commercials soon discover that in order to get work they need a reel. To build a reel, you can either do spec commercials or recut your short into a spec. "I didn't want to bastardize my film," explains *Requiem* director Roy Unger. "But I talked to commercial agencies who said, 'The film's great, but you should figure out a way to make it into a commercial for Playstation or a futuristic high tech product.' If you want to do commercials, you've got to have commercials — that's the bottom line. They don't really want to see anything else. The same thing for the music videos. They want to see music videos on your reel."

IF AT FIRST YOU DON'T SUCCEED...

If you can't parlay your first film into the career you want, make another short. Many filmmakers find they've laid the groundwork with their first short, but industry success came with their second film. If you have the time and money to make another short, and you think you'll get something out of it, do it. You'll discover both making and marketing a short are much easier the second time around. "If you can find a way to make a film within the resources that you can manage, you should always be making something," filmmaker David Birdsell reminds us.

MAKING IT BIG IN SHORTS

By taking an idea for a short film and making it a reality, you've discovered something very important: You can make things happen. Once you understand that your dreams and ambitions are nothing but a series of ideas that you need to turn into reality, you'll recognize that you already have the skills necessary to "produce" your idealized future. Dream of getting into Sundance? Fill out the entry form. Want to win an Academy Award? Qualify for a nomination. If you don't get into Sundance or win an Oscar with your first short, you might succeed with your second. Or third. It's just a matter of getting through the nos until you get a yes. Want an agent? Think organically. Look around. Who do you know who has an agent already? Ask them to refer you. Why should their agent want to represent you? Because you're a talented filmmaker who is going to go far. Be an egoist. You can make anything you want happen. Nothing is harder than making a short film that you can be proud of. Everything else is easy.

TWO FINAL TIPS FOR SUREFIRE SUCCESS

Filmmaker Mark Osborne: "Make shorts that are true to your voice, to what makes you special as a filmmaker. That's your best chance of getting noticed, that's your best chance of getting an audience, that's your best chance of being unique. When I was teaching at Cal Arts, that's what I'd always say. Don't worry about getting a job. Don't worry what anyone else is doing. Don't worry about competing. Just figure out what's special about you and follow through on that."

Filmmaker Eileen O'Meara: "Do exactly what you want to do. Follow your vision. And enjoy the process. Because you never know what's going to happen. So you might as well enjoy it."

SHORT RECAP

- Make a short that best represents you and what you can do.

- Always have at least a few projects that you want to do next.

- If you want to be a Hollywood filmmaker, go to Hollywood.

- If you want to be a commercial or music video director, make spec ads or videos.

- You're a short filmmaker. You can have the skills to make any dream come true. What are you waiting for? Make it happen!

NOTES

[p ix] The Fox Movie Channel still exists, but the short films are no longer played on air.

[p ix] Although the company that produced them is no longer around, the various *Short* and *International Release* DVDs can still be bought on Amazon.

[p ix] I created the "Making and Marketing the Short Film" class in 2000. If you're interested in taking the class, it's now being offered online via UCLA Extension.

[p ix] "Why isn't any": Anonymous audience member from 2002, this book is for you!

[p x] two directors: Thank you, Francine McDougall and Jessica Yu, for everything!

[p x] nominated for an Oscar: Josh Gordon and Will Speck, who made *Angry Boy* for Fox Movie Channel, were nominated for their subsequent live action short, *Culture.*

[p xi] "Kim not only": E-mail correspondence with Lexi Alexander, June 4 2003.

[p 3] Celebrating his twelfth: All information about Jack Nicholson's appreciation of short filmmaking from Julian Schnabel's conversation with Jack Nicholson. Julian Schnabel, "Jack Nicholson Interview," *Interview,* April 2003, p. 153.

[p 4] "One of the most common excuses": Telephone interview with Robbie Consing, May 23, 2003. All quotes from Robbie Consing are from this interview.

[p 4] In 2003, the Sundance Film Festival: Geoffrey Berskshire, "Shorts Make 'Dance Card," *Daily Variety,* 2002.

[p 5] George Lucas's USC piece, *Electronic Labyrinth: THX 1138 4EB* can be seen on DVD on *Short 10: Chaos* (Warner Home Video, 2000).

[p 6] The BMW shorts can be seen on the web site www.bmwfilms.com or on the DVD *BMWfilms.Com Presents The Hire,* Vol. 1, BMW of North America, 2003.

[p 6] Sarah Polley's filmmaking roster includes *All I Want for Christmas* (2002), *I Shout Love* (2001), *The Best Day of My Life* (1999), and *Don't Think Twice* (1999). Rachel Griffiths wrote and directed the shorts *Roundabout* (2002) and *Tulip* (1998).

[p 7] "It's tough to break into filmmaking": In-person interview with David Birdsell, February 26, 2003. All quotes from David Birdsell are from this interview.

[p 15] The Academy of Motion Pictures definition is from the "70th Annual Academy Awards Special Rules for the Short Film Awards," which states running time cannot exceed forty minutes including credits.

[p 15] The MediaTrip definition is from MediaTrip's submission form.

[p 15] The AtomShockwave definition is from the web site submission form.

[p 15] The Independent Film Channel definition is from a previously published IFC web site information form.

[p 15] The Sundance Film Festival definitions are from the 2003 online submission form.

[p 16] "When a short goes over": Telephone interview with Thomas Harris, April 29, 2003. All quotes from Thomas Harris are from this interview.

[p 16] "My first film was": In-person interview with Amy Talkington, May 27, 2003. All quotes from Amy Talkington are from this interview.

[p 16] "Think about it": Telephone interview with George Langworthy, June 3, 2003. All quotes from George Langworthy are from this interview.

[p 16] "It's twelve minutes": Telephone interview with Brian McDonald, June 15, 2003. All quotes from Brian McDonald are from this interview.

[p 17] "I started telling": In-person interview with Mat Fuller, June 6, 2003. All quotes from Mat Fuller are from this interview.

[p 17] "I get a lot of filmmakers": Telephone interview with David Russell, May 26, 2003. All quotes from David Russell are from this interview.

[p 17] "Longer is always tougher": Telephone interview with Megan O'Neill, May 30, 2003. All quotes from Megan O'Neill are from this interview.

[p 17] *Five Feet High and Rising*, along with a companion piece made by director Peter Sollett before he made the feature film *Raising Victor Vargas*, is available on *Short 10: Chaos* (Warner Home Video, 2000).

[p 18] The number of shorts on the web is anyone's guess, but John Halecky of IFILM thinks ten grand is a good ballpark number.

[p 18] A collection of David Lynch's student work and other shorts is available on DVD. Jane Campion's shorter works are for sale via the distributor Women Make Movies. Tim Burton's notorious *Frankenweenie* can be found on VHS. Robert Rodriguez's *Bedhead* is on the Director's Double Feature DVD version of *El Mariachi/Desperado*.

[p 19] "What I like best": Telephone interview with Trevor Groth, December 2001. All quotes from Trevor Groth are from this interview.

[p 19] To the best of my knowledge, *The Lunch Date* is not available commercially. If you're ever in Los Angeles, make an appointment with the Academy of Motion Pictures Arts & Sciences to view the film in their library.

[p 21] "Oddly, when I initially made *More*": Telephone interview with Mark Osborne, June 10, 2003. All quotes from Mark Osbourne are from this interview.

[p 21] "There's been such a huge": Telephone interview with Carol Crowe, President of Apollo Cinema, February 26, 2003. All quotes from Carol Crowe are from this interview.

[p 22] *Entertainment Weekly's* Top 50 Cult Film issue is dated May 23, 2003.

[p 23] "If you strip it down": Telephone interview with Joel S. Bachar, founder of Independent Exposure, May 28, 2003. All quotes from Joel S. Bachar are from this interview.

[p 24] "Filmmakers enjoy the joke": E-mail correspondence with producer Michael Wiese, May 30, 2003.

[p 25] Lou Harris, Editor, *The IFILM Internet Movie Guide*, (Hollywood: Lone Eagle Publishing Company, 2002).

[p 25] All information about *405* is garnered from the film's web site FAQ.

[p 28] "It's a short film" In-person conversation with Noah Edelson circa 1997 (his festival circuit year).

[p 28] "I had fun doing a piece": E-mail correspondence with Eileen O'Meara, May 26, 2003.

[p 29] "Most people they": Telephone interview with Mark Borchardt, June 5, 2003. All quotes from Mark Borchardt are from this interview.

[p 29] "The best thing about short": Telephone interview with Karl T. Hirsch, June 1, 2003. All quotes from Karl T. Hirsch are from this interview.

[p 33] All information about *El Mariachi* taken from Rodriguez's *10 Minute Film School* bonus feature on the Director's Double Feature DVD version of *El Mariachi/Desperado*.

[p 49] "Aside from being Sam Mendes": E-mail correspondence from Bob Mandel, June 6, 2003.

[p 51] "I was co-producing": Discussion board posting by Melissa Brantley, UCLA Extension online course, "Making and Marketing the Short Film," July 2003.

[p 52] "so freakin' stressed": Discussion board posting by Jordan Horowitz, UCLA Extension online course, "Making and Marketing the Short Film," July 2003. All quotes from Jordan Horowitz are from his discussion board postings.

[p 55] All information on *Gasline* is gleaned from the 2002 Sundance Film Festival online catalogue filmmaker pages.

[p 55] "At IFILM, we would": Telephone interview with John Halecky, December 2001. All quotes from John Halecky are from this interview.

[p 56] Although *Troops* isn't yet on DVD (except for a free insert DVD made by the magazine *Total Movie*), both *Hardware Wars* (Michael Wiese Productions, 2002) and *George Lucas in Love* (Red Hill, 2000) are available for sale on DVD.

[p 59] *Saving Ryan's Privates* can be seen on www.atomfilms.com.

[p 63] David Birsell's first film, the USC short *Blue City* (Sundance Film Festival, 1997), is available on *Short 6: Insanity* (Warner Home Video, 1999). His second short, shot on that street, is the Fox Movie Short, *Phil Touches Flo* (Sundance Film Festival, 1998). The photo of this street was taken by Birdsell when he did his storyboards with photographs rather than drawings.

[p 63] *Multifacial* is available on *Short 5: Diversity* (Warner Home Video, 1999).

[p 63] *Pig!* can be seen on *www.ifilm.com.*

[p 63] "if you want to make short," Telephone conversation with Roy Unger, June 10, 2003. All quotes from Roy Unger are from this interview.

[p 64] "Something that is going": In-person interview with Tara Veneruso, February 27, 2003. All quotes from Tara Veneruso are from this interview.

[p 67] The Academy acknowledges IMAX theaters in the 70th Annual Academy Awards Special Rules for the Short Film Awards.

[p 74] *Nadja* was issued on DVD by Pioneer Video in 2000. *The Rocking Horse Winner* is not commercially available at this time.

[p 74] "lets kids create": Found on original packaging of a camera sold on eBay.

[p 80] "Film prints will": E-mail correspondence with Don Hertzfeldt, June 9, 2003.

[p 87] "Here we are": From notes taken at Danny Simon's writing class, Sherman Oaks, CA, 1991.

[p 96] Actually, we scored two pugs — for the price of one. The one in the publicity photo in this chapter is the pug that played Frank the Alien in both *Men in Black* films.

[p 100] *Phil Touches Flo* was made in 1997; the prices reflect that.

[p 146] "Burners are relatively": Telephone interview with Jess Bowers, June 6, 2003. All quotes from Jess Bowers are from this interview.

[p 152] Mara Schwartz can always be counted on to generously share this information with my UCLA Extension class.

[p 160] "We've managed fifty-seven": E-mail correspondence with Jeff Bemiss, May 26, 2003.

[p 164] "Selling the t-shirts": E-mail correspondence with Ari Gold, *www.arigoldfilms.com*, May 28, 2003. The shirts are still available for sale on his web site! Copies of his film are as well.

[p 170] *I Killed My Lesbian Wife* is available to see on www.AtomShockwave.com and *deleriouspink* is on the DVD *Short 10: Chaos.*

[p 171] The 50% U.S. financing rule is according to the 2004 Sundance Film Festival application.

[p 173] "This is Culture": www.arigoldfilms.com.

[p 173] "Peace by way of Hell": Epiphany postcard. Director: Arayna Thomas. ISIS Productions, LLC. *http://www.isisproductions.net.*

[p 174] "The film must be": You can read more about *Culture* and even watch it in its one-minute entirety on www.arigoldfilms.com.

[p 183] 3,345 shorts: Geoffrey Berskshire, "Shorts Make 'Dance Card," Daily Variety, 2002.

[p 193] "Flickerfest in Australia": Telephone interview with Sandrine Cassidy, May 28, 2003.

[p 195] "My short": E-mail correspondence with Douglas Horn, May 28, 2003.

[p 202] "As animation continues": E-mail correspondence with Don Hertzfeldt, July 2003.

[p 203] "CustomFlix launched a new": E-mail correspondence with Darren Giles, July 2003.

PHOTO AND ILLUSTRATION CREDITS:

[p vii] On the set of *Coven*. Courtesy of Mark Borchardt. Photographer: Chris Smith.

[p ix] On the set of *Phil Touches Flo*. Photographer: Suzanne Hanover.

[p x] Publicity still from *deleriouspink*. Courtesy of Sebastian del Castillo. Photographer: Andrew Busti.

[p xi] Kyle Heath Leppert looks into a mini-DV camera. Photographer: Kim Adelman.

[p xi] Publicity still from *One Hand Left*. Photographer: Suzanne Hanover.

[p 3] Publicity still from *Deveria*. Courtesy of Mat Fuller. Photographer: Mike Witherspoon.

[p 5] Amber Montervino checks out the Canon Zoom 250 Super-8 camera. Photographer: Kim Adelman.

[p 10] Musicians rock. Photographer: Craig Adelman.

[p 15] Publicity still from *More*. Courtesy of Mark Osborne, www.happyproduct.com.

[p 20] Publicity still from Jane Campion's *Peel*. Courtesy of Women Make Movies.

[p 27] On the set of *Sidewalkers*. Courtesy of Tara Veneruso. Photographer: Lance Mungia.

[p 33] On the set of *Beeker's Crossing*. Photographer: Sylvia Abumuhor.

[p 34] On the set of *Bad Animals*. Photographer: Mark Skoner.

[p 38] On the set of *H@*. Photographer: Sylvia Abumuhor.

[p 41] Shaun Young looks through the Canon XL1 eyepiece. Photographer: Kim Adelman.

[p 50] On the set of *Birthday*. Photographer: Sylvia Abumuhor.

[p 55] *Hardware Wars* DVD cover. Courtesy of Michael Wiese.

[p 63] The street that inspired *Phil Touches Flo*. Photographer: David Birdsell.

[p 67] Ted Williams handles a borrowed Sony mini-DV cam. Photographer: Kim Adelman.

[p 69] Phillippa Rick looks through the Ultravision 35mm camera eyepiece. Photographer: Suzanne Hanover.

[p 73] Lisa Daniels peers through a vintage Yashica 25 Super-8. Photographer: Kim Adelman.

[p 77] On the set of *Bad Animals*. Photographer: Mark Skoner.

[p 79] Kyle Heath Leppert looks into the mini-DV camera viewfinder. Photographer: Kim Adelman.

[p 81] Wendy Rothman knows the value of a tripod. Photographer: Kim Adelman.

[p 85] *Five Puppies on the Run* storyboard by Lauren Beaumont, age eight.

[p 91] *I'm on Fire* storyboard by Ryan Rowe.

[p 93] Robbie Consing on the set of *Beeker's Crossing*. Photographer: Suzanne Hanover.

[p 95] On the set of *Bad Animals*. Photographer: Mark Skoner.

[p 100] Publicity still from *Phil Touches Flo*. Photographer: Suzanne Hanover.

[p 107] On the set of *Birthday*. Photographer: Sylvia Abumuhor.

[p 109] On the set of *Deveria*. Photographer: Mike Witherspoon.

[p 110] On the set of *Beeker's Crossing*. Photographer: Sylvia Abumuhor.

[p 116] On the set of *Bad Animals*. Photographer: Mark Skoner.

[p 119] On the set of *Hope Street*. Photographer: Suzanne Hanover.

[p 122] On the set of *Sidewalkers*. Photographer: Lance Mungia.

[p 129] On the set of *A Fine Day for Flying*. Photographer: Sylvia Abumuhor.

[p 135] Filmmaker Tara Veneruso edits on her own system. Photographer: Kim Adelman.

[p 140] Director Eugenia Ives supervises sound work on *Ladies Room*. Photographer: Kim Adelman.

[p 149] Ask a band like Delta 72 to score your movie. Photographer: Craig Adelman.

[p 154] Composer Matt Cartsonis. Photographer: Kim Adelman.

[p 159] Noah Edelson touches Jessica Yu's Oscar. Photographer: Amy Jurist.

[p 164] Own your own *Culture* T-shirt. Available at www.arigoldfilms.com. Photographer: Kim Adelman.

[p 169] *Requiem* man. Courtesy of Roy Unger.

[p 177] *Media Whore* postcard. Courtesy of Aglet Productions. Photographer: Ramon Estrada.

[p 181] Robert Redford networks at the 1997 Sundance Film Festival. Photographer: Noah Edelson.

[p 196] Filmmakers Michael Schlitt and Alex Metcalf socialize at the Palm Springs International Festival of Short Films. Photographer: Kim Adelman.

[p 199] Publicity still from *Rejected*. Courtesy of Don Hertzfeldt.

[p 213] Going Hollywood. Photographer: Kim Adelman.

[p 218] Going Sundance. Photographer: Bear Fisher.

[p 251] Author photo. Photographer: Carol Sheridan.

INDEX

ACKNOWLEDGMENTS

The author wishes to thank (in alphabetical order):

Sylvia Abumuhor, Kevin Ackerman, Derth Adams, Molly-Dodd Wheeler Adams, Craig Adelman, Howard Adelman, Nancy Adelman, Lexi Alexander, Robin Alper, Dominique Arcadio, Elena Arroy, Jamie Babbit, Joel S. Bachar, Aparna Bakhle, Carin Baer, Shanin Michelle Beard, Lauren Beaumont, Spencer Beglarian, Nina Berry, David Birdsell, Scott Boettle, Mark Borchardt, Mark Steven Bosco, Jess Bowers, Melissa Brantley, Greg Brooker, Kimberley Browning, Maria Burton, Andrew Busti, Patrice Callahan, Jane Campion, Colin Campbell, Steve Carcano, Robert Carrasco, Matt Cartsonis, Susan Cartsonis, Sandrine Faucher Cassidy, Andrew Crane, Michele Chong, Curtis Choy, William Clark, Lilli Cloud, Robert Cobb, Peet Cocke, Becky Cole, Keiann Collins, Robbie Consing, Charles Cook, John Cooper, Jan Cox, Jeff Cox, Andrew Crane, Carol Crowe, Carmen Cuba, Lisa Daniels, Bob Davis, Russell DeGrazier, Greg Dellerson, Maria de la Torre, Sebastian del Castillo, Jim Denault, Jennifer Derwingson, Balinda DeSantis, John Dickson, Chip Diggins, Leslie Dinaberg, Dan Dubiecki, Guy Dyas, Christine Ecklund, Noah Edelson, Martin Etchart, Chris Fahland, Victor Fannuchi, Tai Fauci, Debbie Felton, Bear Fisher, Kathleen French, Brenda Friend, Mat Fuller, Glenn Gaylord, Natalie Gildea, Terry Gilliam, Ari Gold, Jelani Gould-Bailey, Josh Gordon, Linda Gordon, Bennett Graebner, Trevor Groth, Shana Hagan, Bryan Hale, Billy Hall, Suzanne Hanover, Thomas Ethan Harris, Gavin Harvey, Kevin Hassaurad, Jim Healy, Carol Heikkinen, Eleo Hensleigh, Don Hertzfeldt, Karl Hirsch, Douglas Horn, Jordan Horowitz, Mike Horowitz, Anne Hubbell, Jeremy Hunt, Doug "Disco" Hylton, Larry Hymes, Eugenia Ives, Andre Jacquemetton, Maria Jacquemetton, Deb Jarnes, Liz Jereski, Allan Johnson, Sara Juarez, Amy Jurist, Caroline Kaplan, Howard Karesh, Nancy Keystone, David King, Samuel Kivi, Zak Klobucher, David Koff, Tony Kountz, John Lehr, George Langworthy, Gail Lerner, Ellie Lee, Ken Lee, Sunny Lee, Kyle Heath Leppert, Joel Leslie, Lorraine LoBianco, Todd Longwell, Bob Mandel, Holly Mandel, Lance Mungia, Karen Mann, Chris Marker, Carol May, Brian McConnell, Brian McDonald, William McDonald, Francine McDougall, Genevieve McGillicuddy, Andrew Mersmann, Alex Metcalf, Joel Metzger, Clinton Miguel, Loren Miller, Dean Minerd, William Mochon, Ron Modro, Tony Molina, Amber Montervino, William Morosi, Frank Morris,

Robert Morris, Meg Moynihan, Andrew Mudge, Brent Muscay, Jessie Nagel, Jamie Neese, Marni Nelko, Louise Neibold, Sandra Neufeldt, Steven Nily, Matt Nix, Paul Norlen, Austin Olah, Susan O'Leary, Kimberly Olivo, Colleen O'Mara, Eileen O'Meara, Megan O'Neill, Lorne Orleans, Mark Osborne, Lynn Padilla, Raena Padilla, Greg Pak, Nicholas Panoutsopoulos, Jeff Payne, David Pearlman, Bob Pederson, Laura Phillips, Stacey Pianko, Tracy Nan Pion, Romen Podzyhun, Michael Price, Cynthia Pusheck, Greg Pyros, Corky Quakenbush, Linda Quakenbush, Doris Quon, Leslie Rabb, Abu Rasheduzzaman, Robert Redford, Allison Reeds, Jason Reitman, Kenny Rhodes, Phillippa Rick, Michael Rivkin, David Rooney, Billy Rose, Anne Rosellini, Andrew Rosen, Douglas Ross, Wendy Rothman, Ryan Rowe, Dave Rudd, David Russell, Edward Saile, Ralph Sall, Mika Salmi, Mike Schwab, Mara Schwartz, Michael Schlitt, Marliese Schneider, Rick Scott, Kimberly Sharp, Linda Sheetz, Carol Sheridan, Katie Shiban, Ricardo Nobuo Shima, Tricia Stewart Shiu, Lesley Marlene Siegel, Danny Simon, Jason Simon, Kelly Simpson, Monika Skerbelis, Mark Skoner, Paul Skorich, Leslie Kollins Small, Alex Smith, Andrew Smith, Cat Chapman Smith, Roger Smith, Shane Smith, Mark Sonnenberg, Will Speck, Sarah Stanley, Jennifer Stark, John Starr, Eric Steelberg, Jonathon Sterns, Greg Stewart, Mark Stolaroff, Amy Talkington, Cathy Tanzer, John Teska, Laura Thielen, Arayna Thomas, Betsy Thomas, Beth Hall Thrasher, Gabe Torres, Colby Tseng, Roy Unger, Peggy Van Norman, Amanda Veith, Tara Veneruso, Pat Verducci, Stuart Voytilla, Morrie Warshawski, Andrew Weiner, Richard Weiss, Chris Wells, Craig Wells, Jakob White, Jason White, Michael Wiese, Bergen Williams, Doug Williams, Rob Williams, Ted Williams, Holly Willis, Chad Wilson, Wendy Wilson, Alison Winward, Mike Witherspoon, Women Make Movies, Mark Wynns, Jamie Wynns, Kathie Fong Yoneda, Shaun Young, and Jessica Yu.

ABOUT THE AUTHOR

Kim Adelman currently teaches "Making and Marketing the Short Film" at UCLA Extension. She began her short film career by launching the Fox Movie Channel's short film program in 1996. The nineteen short films she produced for Fox won thirty-plus awards and played over one hundred and fifty film festivals worldwide, including the Sundance Film Festival four years in a row. Adelman then signed on to produce *Short* and *International Release*, the acclaimed short film compilations issued on DVD by Warner Home Video. The impressive roster of filmmakers whose shorts were released on those DVDs includes George Lucas, Jane Campion, Chris Marker, Guy Maddin, Mark Osborne, Don Hertzfeldt, Amy Talkington, David Birdsell, Eileen O'Meara, Peter Sollett, Saul Bass, Alain Resnais, Agnès Varda, Charles Stone III, Greg Pak, Leni Riefenstahl, and Charles and Ray Eames. In addition to speaking at countless film festivals, she has written articles about the short film world for ifilm.com and AIVF's *The Independent* magazine. Ms. Adelman is also the author of two pop culture books, *The Girls' Guide to Elvis* and *The Girls' Guide to Country*. She can be reached at *www.kimadelman.com.*

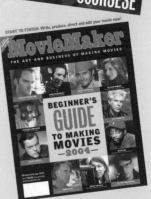

THE WRITER'S JOURNEY
2nd Edition
Mythic Structure for Writers

Christopher Vogler

Over 116,000 sold!

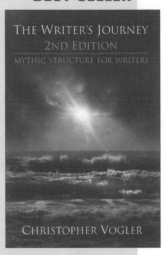

See why this book has become an international bestseller and a true classic. *The Writer's Journey* explores the powerful relationship between mythology and storytelling in a clear, concise style that's made it required reading for movie executives, screenwriters, playwrights, scholars, and fans of pop culture all over the world.

Both fiction and nonfiction writers will discover a set of useful myth-inspired storytelling paradigms (i.e., "The Hero's Journey") and step-by-step guidelines to plot and character development. Based on the work of Joseph Campbell, *The Writer's Journey* is a must for all writers interested in further developing their craft.

The updated and revised second edition provides new insights and observations from Vogler's ongoing work on mythology's influence on stories, movies, and man himself.

"This book is like having the smartest person in the story meeting come home with you and whisper what to do in your ear as you write a screenplay. Insight for insight, step for step, Chris Vogler takes us through the process of connecting theme to story and making a script come alive."
> — Lynda Obst, Producer
> *Sleepless in Seattle, How to Lose a Guy in 10 Days*
> Author, *Hello, He Lied*

Christopher Vogler, a top Hollywood story consultant and development executive, has worked on such high-grossing feature films as *The Lion King* and conducts writing workshops around the globe.

$24.95 | 325 pages | Order #98RLS | ISBN: 0-941188-70-1

24 HOURS | **1.800.833.5738** | **www.mwp.com**

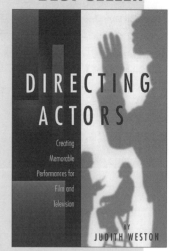

ORDER FORM

MICHAEL WIESE PRODUCTIONS
11288 VENTURA BLVD., # 621
STUDIO CITY, CA 91604
E-MAIL: MWPSALES@MWP.COM
WEB SITE: WWW.MWP.COM

WRITE OR FAX FOR A FREE CATALOG

PLEASE SEND ME THE FOLLOWING BOOKS:

TITLE	ORDER NUMBER (#RLS _____)	AMOUNT
	SHIPPING	
	CALIFORNIA TAX (8.00%)	
	TOTAL ENCLOSED	

PLEASE MAKE CHECK OR MONEY ORDER PAYABLE TO:

MICHAEL WIESE PRODUCTIONS

(CHECK ONE) _____ MASTERCARD _____ VISA _____ AMEX

CREDIT CARD NUMBER _____

EXPIRATION DATE _____

CARDHOLDER'S NAME _____

CARDHOLDER'S SIGNATURE _____

SHIP TO:

NAME _____

ADDRESS _____

CITY _____ STATE _____ ZIP _____

COUNTRY _____ TELEPHONE _____